THE SUM OF THE PARTS

Erratic Episodes

Jack Rosenthal

CONTENTS

INTRODUCTION

Unpredictability can be one of life's excitements: you just never know what might happen next. It is also of course the main cause of our insecurities. That it's a good thing we don't know what's around the corner is a self-evident truth.

On balance unpredictability is best enjoyed in retrospect once we've dealt with its outcomes. So that's what this is: a random recollection of episodes from a life that spanned the second half of the twentieth century. Not to imply that much, or any, reference is made to the momentous national and global events that occurred in those decades of seismic change. Rather I hope in total it might give a sense of just one life lived through that time. I hope the reading will give as much pleasure as did the remembering.

COMMON FEAR

My mother didn't like Alsatian dogs. She saw them as Germans. Too untrustworthy she said (she was born two years after the Treaty of Versailles and the Germans killed her brother in 1944). But my own dislike didn't need her encouragement. The two Alsatians Jimmy Atkins kept on the Common had always been creatures of mythic terror to us village children.

At five or six years old we saw the green billows of prickly gorse and heather stretching away behind our homes much as early navigators must have seen the green swells of the Atlantic: beckoning. The difference was that in the distant top corner of the Common, where the gorse gave way to birch and bracken, lay not the New World of Canada or New England but Jimmy's Acre. And instead of dragons patrolling the edge of the known world, Jimmy's Alsatians. Quite how Jimmy had managed to establish his own private colony on this piece of supposedly commonly held property was not recorded but nobody seemed to mind. He kept pigs on it in a dilapidation of rusting tin huts. The perimeter of his land-grab was marked by rusty wire netting supported on lengths of angle iron and bits of derelict bedstead, all guarded by the two Alsatians. Creeping forward on hands and knees through the bracken we would play chicken, exchanging whispered dares to run right up to the sagging wire we were certain was incapable of stopping the enraged charge of two slavering wolf-dogs intent on eating us.

As it was the dogs might have been truly mythic because

we never actually saw them. We always assumed they must have been sleeping inside one of the huts. Even when, in a fit of bravado, 'Whizzer' Goodwin once ran forward and shouted through the wire "I in't afraid o' no Jerry dogs!" nothing happened above a few extra grunts from the pigs, though we fled like rabbits through the gorse, scratching our bare legs to blood. The proof that Jimmy's Alsatians really did exist came about in an unusual way.

Not far from Jimmy's Acre was Moody's Hole. This was an old sandpit grown round with gorse and it was crucial to Moody Bloomfield's contract with the Leiston Town Council. In those early years after the war Leiston had a population of around twelve thousand but an infrastructure that did not yet offer universal drainage. Many of its citizens still made use of buckets in outhouses and, as not everyone had the garden space to safely deploy the contents of these buckets on a sustainable basis, particularly where the domestic water supply came from an adjacent well, Moody's services were essential to the town's well-being. While Leiston's milkmen were still getting dressed a pungent smell, the clang of a metal lid and the clop of hooves in the dark would signal Moody's progress through the streets of Victorian terraces as the waiting buckets of 'night soil' were tipped into a horse-drawn cart designed for the purpose.

In another society this aggregated material might have been considered of value for manurial purposes but Moody never developed the recycling option. Perhaps the local agriculturists were too squeamish. Instead the content of the cart was tipped into Moody's Hole on the Common where it would soak away into the sand, at least until the accumulated solids sealed the strata. Thereafter a fetid pool would appear, deepening and widening with each further load. Eventually Moody would be obliged, in the interests of public if not personal hygiene, to arm himself with a bailing bucket and a spade before descending into the hole to square and deepen it to absorb the effluent more effectively.

Moody had not acquired his name from any deep-seated sadness, understandable though that might have been given the nature of his profession, but more because of his implacable terseness of speech. This was illustrated one cold February morning at the offices of the Leiston Town Council. On a Tuesday, after finishing his round, Moody would return to his cottage, unhitch the empty cart, turn out the pony to graze and eat a nourishing breakfast of kippers brought by the fish man on Mondays (a strong constitution was obviously a pre-requisite of the job). After this early breakfast he would cycle into Leiston to collect his wages from Mrs Woolnough, the town's bookkeeper and treasurer. On this morning he was half an hour later than usual.

"Good morning Mr Bloomfield" said Mrs Woolnough "you're a little later than normal. It must have been a bit icy earlier?"

"No" said Moody.

Knowing that the town clock could be set by Moody's punctuality Mrs Woolnough probed.

"Is everything all right?"

"Yis" said Moody.

Mrs Woolnough persevered.

"Well you're not normally late Mr Bloomfield."

Interpreting this as a rebuke Moody felt obliged to explain.

"Me wife was taken queer in the night."

"Oh I am sorry," said Mrs Woolnough "what happened?"

"Oi had t' git the doctor in the finish" said Moody "'n then oi had t'git me own kippers." This was the longest sentence Mrs Woolnough, or indeed anyone, had ever heard Moody speak.

"Did the doctor say what was wrong?" asked Mrs Woolnough.

"No he d'int" said Moody.

"Well here's this week's money Mr Bloomfield, and I do hope your wife gets better very soon" said Mrs Woolnough, realising there was little point in further pursuit.

"She 'ont" said Moody taking the proffered envelope from Mrs Woolnough's hand and turning to leave.

"Oh dear, what makes you say that?" asked Mrs Woolnough.

"She died" said Moody closing the door behind him and leaving Mrs Woolnough somewhat stunned.

The presence of Jimmy's Acre and Moody's Hole meant the far edge of the Common was a fearful region for us small children. Not so for the wild offspring of the gypsies who pitched up on the Common every summer. We kept apart so they knew nothing of our small terrors but had they, they had would have accorded them no weight. Their parents were old-fashioned travellers with piebald ponies pulling small, ornately painted wagons with bowtop roofs and projecting stove pipes. They tethered the ponies on the velvety grass oasies of the rabbit lawns amid the gorse and threw up tents of greasy canvas around the site of their nightly campfires. The children, dark and lithe, their lean faces smeared with wood ash, would scamper through the gorse on blackened feet inured to the prickles, an ability wondrous to us pink-fleshed softies. The wiry men sought work in the fields by day and took their lurchers out by night. Their black-haired women, wrapped in yards of skirt and scarf, knocked at the back doors of the village hawking split wooden clothes pegs and willow baskets. They spoke their own strange language and conducted deals with hand-signs and numbers articulated in heavy accents. There was an air of mystery and old country romance about them. At night their fires would flicker on the Common and through bedroom windows open to summer warmth we could sometimes hear the strains of a fiddle.

With stories of kidnappings and slave sales to far off lands our grandparents and parents would warn us to keep away from these unkempt visitors. Yet our fears were tempered by exciting dreams of a life on the road beyond the reach of school and authority. Inevitably the gypsies were assumed to be the perpetrators of any local misdemeanours, particularly theft, and some permanent local residents were not slow to take advantage of the prejudice.

Jimmy's Alsatians were intended as a deterrent to gypsies or anyone else who might fancy roast pork and crackling as an alternative to rabbit pie or carrot and Oxo stew. The temptation was real, for in the early 1950s the country was only slowly pulling away from decades of depression and wartime privation. Rationing continued. Each Saturday morning Mr Baker, the Leiston grocer, would tear off the coupons from my granny's ration book to validate the small cardboard box of provisions he left on her kitchen table. Once, as the result of a deal involving some parsnip wine and boiled bacon, my grandmother came into the possession of two dead cockerels. One was served to the family the following Sunday, the other was carefully packed and posted to my aunt in London as a rare commodity of considerable value. So owning half a dozen sows and their growing litters up on the Common clearly made Jimmy Atkins a man of notable assets. Unfortunately for Jimmy their canine protection force was not up to the job.

After the loss of his wife people began to notice that Moody was becoming more loquacious than he had been. Not that he became garrulous but he did start to acknowledge greetings from passers by with a word or two rather than with the imperceptible dip of his chin which, at best, had been his previous reaction. He did not suddenly begin to volunteer information or opinions but he would return a 'Mornin'' or a 'How do'. Thus Jimmy Atkins, on his way up to feed his pigs early one morning was only a little astonished when Moody, returning from the Hole, pulled his pony to a stop to address him.

"They in't there" said Moody

"Wot in't?" responded Jimmy

"Yer pigs"

"Wot d'yer mean in't there?"

"Wot I say"

"Where are they then?"

"Gorn"

"Gorn where?"

"Runned orf"

"Where are the dogs then?"

"In the Hole"

At which Jimmy broke into a trot up the track and Moody flicked his reins to re-start the pony.

The first thing Jimmy saw was the six-foot high wire gate to his enclosure sagging wide open and beyond it all the doors of the tin pigsties standing ajar. Ignoring this catastrophe he ran on to the edge of Moody's Hole, cautiously approached its lip and peered down. There on the surface of the stinking slime floated the sodden bodies of the two Alsatians, partially covered with the latest deposit from Moody's cart. The dogs were clearly dead so Jimmy's next move was to look for his pigs. Distant grunts and squeals led him to the top edge of the Common where the gorse gave way to the arable fields of Bulls Hall. In a field of turnips were the pigs, or at least some of them, having the time of their lives.

Anyone who has tried to herd excited pigs will know that directing cats is a lot easier. Jimmy spent the rest of that day and most of the next rounding them up. Even so over the next week reports kept coming in of various sized pigs spotted free ranging across neighbouring parishes. And of course it was not everyone who would rush to report the fortuitous appearance of a pig. When all the dust had settled Jimmy reckoned he was at least a dozen well-grown weaners and one sow short, not to mention the sad end encountered by his dogs. His first thought had been to drag the dogs clear of the filth of the Hole for the sake of decency and proper interment. The reality of what that would involve persuaded Jimmy that pragmatism was the better part of valour and the two carcasses were left to dissolve and sink into the stinking mire. It did not take long.

Who had inflicted this disaster on the likeable Jimmy? What had killed the dogs? The balance of village opinion held that they must have been poisoned and that the people who knew most about poisons, potions and such like were of course the gypsies. But there had been no gypsies on the Common at the time. Eventually the finger of suspicion pointed toward an immigrant Irish labourer with whom Jimmy had argued about a garden fence but nothing was ever proven and the culprit remained unknown.

Moody carried on with his odious round and monosyllabic greetings until the extension of the Leiston sewage works and the coming of modern septic tanks finally finished his career in the mid-'50s. After the incident on the Common Jimmy threw in his hand with pigs and dogs, concentrating instead on restoring and maintaining his steam traction engine. With this he worked as a jobbing ploughman, turning the soil of various allotments and smallholdings around the neighbourhood. His amenable character had not been embittered by the loss of his livestock but afterwards some people thought they could detect a slight narrowing of his eyes when he conversed, as if to focus a faint glimmer of an ever-present suspicion. His acre on the Common quickly became submerged under an explosive growth of birch and bramble fuelled by the legacy of its previous occupants.

The summer visits of the gypsies became more sporadic: sometimes they appeared but more often they did not as the old traveller tradition died, eroded by motorised vehicles and new ways of living.

A BEDROOM OWL

On the opposite side of the Common from Jimmy's Acre was the Mill House where my great grandfather Charlie Thorpe lived with his wife Alice. Well into the 1950s they managed without the benefit of electricity, thinking it far too dangerous to have indoors. They slept in a brass bed that Alice kept gleaming and when she carried up a candle at bedtime the four polished spheres that ornamented its head and foot reflected the flickering light as if at the entrance to some exotic bazaar. From the gloom of the wall high above the bed a mounted barn owl gazed down, its pale heart-shaped face now and then catching the wan light like some hovering spirit struggling to become incarnate.

Charlie's father, my great, great grandfather, had given Charlie and Alice the owl when they married in 1891. It had come with the whispered information that if it were installed in the marital bedroom only male children would be conceived in its presence. That suited Charlie well enough for strapping sons were what he needed to help on the farm. At first he had put it on the wall opposite the head of the bed but Alice had found its unblinking stare discomfiting. So Charlie had moved it to its final position above the bed where Alice could not see it once she was settled. Subsequently they had two sons, Clifford, and George, my grandfather.

In 1957 Charlie died of bowel cancer and the lonely, grief-stricken Alice followed soon after. The Mill House, still without electricity, was cleared and sold. Knowing I had always been fascinated by, and was not a little fearful of the bedroom owl, my parents passed it to me, a stuffed bird having no place amid the modern décor of our London flat. Perhaps they thought to allay my childish fears by giving me possession of the Victorian relic. Certainly sitting on a formica table under the bright light of my bedroom it lost much of its foreboding aura. But it deserved better than to be reduced to a sad, mummified corpse rattling with pellets fired from the BB gun I had been given for my ninth birthday.

Decades later, though I revelled in the delight of being father to three wondrous daughters, I sometimes mused on what difference there might have been had the owl been accorded the respect, and the situation, to which it was accustomed.

GUN CONTROL

Perhaps it was because of my American blood that guns played a significant part in my early life, although I hadn't intended shooting the famous writer's baby. I wasn't *that* daft, despite the subsequent suspicions levelled at me. And it has to be admitted I had form. There had been the business with Joanna, and then the fire. Looking back I blame Hopalong Cassidy. Anyone who argues that screen violence does not influence children wasn't living with me in the 1950s.

Hopalong was always blasting encircling redskins off their ponies as if they were tin ducks in a shooting gallery. Or surviving hand-to-hand combat with lone braves (white actors badly made up to look indigenous) who dropped out of trees armed with huge Bowie knives. After a day of such heroics he would relax by a campfire with his sidekick Gabby, a tin plate of smoky beans and some casual platitudes released in a cowboy drawl. I loved it and was desperate to recreate such manly, outdoor heroism in my own small life. I was of course misguided and opportunities were limited. For a start I didn't have a proper gun, there weren't any redskins around in north London and I was never convinced that what my mother assured me were cowboy beans were the real McCoy. On the plus side I did have a sidekick, Rosemary Frew.

Romey and I were primary school tearaways. In another life and time we would have rushed forward to shoplifting and drugs and teenage sex but that was a step too far for eight-year-olds in the '50s. So we made do with torturing Joanna. Like us,

Joanna lived in one of four low blocks of flats that enclosed an acre or two of gardens in our part of West Hampstead. She was lanky and pallid and didn't make friends easily so was prepared to put up with a lot to be allowed to tag around in a threesome. We decided to turn her into a captive Indian squaw which, we insisted, required her to take off all her clothes, necessarily in a location with a low risk of adult interference.

Penetrating far and deep under the gardens a number of tunnel-like air-raid shelters had been excavated during the war. To us their poorly barricaded openings were the portals to Hell. Within, the gloom of receding daylight quickly gave way to a sinister blackness echoing the dripping of water, the scuttling of rats and the slurp of our feet through the mush of what we imagined were decaying bodies. The ideal venue for enslaving a squaw. Joanna was quite happy to go along with our plan, undressing herself and tying on the loincloth I had fashioned from a folded tea towel and some kitchen string. I think it was at this point that Romey and I, who had naturally assumed the superior role of U.S. cavalry, wondered if it might not have been more fun to be the squaw. The whole thing was loaded with pre-pubescent eroticism. But by then Joanna was beginning to look a bit goose-pimpled, especially when we tied her hands behind her back and prodded her down into the blackness with what we thought were appropriate exclamations such as 'Pesky Redskin' and 'Yer headin' back to the Reservation pronto'. We put a noose of dressing gown cord around her neck, looped the other end over a protuberance on an old grass roller we walked into in the dark and went home.

Our knots weren't up to much so Joanna was able to wiggle her hands free to take the noose off her neck and go home too. But by then she was late and when she explained why, her father, just home from the City, didn't think much of it and came to see mine. It would have all blown over as innocent play except Joanna felt she had let the side down by not staying tied up and so was keen to continue playing cowboys and indians the next afternoon rather than suffer our disapproval. With my official sidekick ill in bed I decided on a campfire with beans.

As it was drizzling with rain the obvious campfire site was in one of the individual cellars built into the foundations of the flats. These had basement style doors opening onto the gardens. We soon found one unlocked, replete with kindling and coal. Not being experienced at the lighting of campfires we had difficulty in getting the kindling to do much other than smoke, so we shut the door and went off to look for some dry newspaper. Returning not many minutes later we opened the door onto a roaring inferno. Shocked, our response was to quickly shut the door and run to the playground situated in the middle of the gardens. There we nonchalantly sat rocking on the swings trying not to notice the black smoke beginning to seep into the air from the direction of the cellar. It wasn't long before clanging bells announced the approach of a fire engine. The other children surged off towards it with a wild chorus of 'FIRE FIRE' while Joanna and I wandered homeward with a strong suspicion we might have overdone it this time. Mr Joanna certainly felt we had, pointing out to my father that as the cellar had contained not only wood and coal but also a tank of paraffin the combined effect might well have achieved what Hitler hadn't insofar as our homes were concerned. His wrath culminated in the announcement that I was now banned from any further association with his daughter, which prompted my own father to announce that he had seldom encountered such a disagreeable and irrational man. Good old Dad. Anyway that's what I meant by having incriminating form as it wasn't long after this that the baby shooting thing came up requiring my father to once more leap to my defence.

As a nine-year-old my ambition to become a gunslinger was only slightly advanced by my acquisition of an American-style BB gun. This used a charge of compressed air to propel a small metal ball at minimal velocity but sufficient, at least insofar as my mother kept warning me, to blind someone should it hit their eyeball. Its velocity had certainly been enough to break the glass of the case that had (ineffectually) protected the bedroom owl so callously destroyed.

Despite my treatment of the owl, or possibly in the hope of moving me on to more responsible behaviour, my father agreed to buy me a proper airgun as a concession to my reaching double figure age. A BSA Airsporter. This was very nearly a real gun in that it could actually kill living things- the advertisement I had originally spotted in *The Angling Times* claimed it *'well-suited to vermin control including rabbits'*. As a small ten-year-old I could hardly manage to pull the compression lever down sufficiently far to arm the thing. Clearly this was not a weapon for indoor use but luckily, depending on your subsequent viewpoint, our second-floor flat had a balcony overlooking the gardens. By now I had moved on from Hopalong Cassidy, replacing him with the heroes of Stalag 17 and the Battle of Britain as described weekly in the pages of The *Hotspur* and *The Wizard.* Although the single sharp 'toof' of the Airsporter being fired was a poor substitute for the rat-tat-tat of a Tommy gun, our balcony made for a passable armed watchtower on the perimeter of a German POW camp. The ivy entwined over the balustrading added to the effect by resembling camouflage netting. The real problem was what to shoot at.

As I've said I wasn't so daft as to think shooting at people or babies would be acceptable, although I did always hope I might spot a daylight burglar climbing in through a ground floor window. In which case I would become an instant hero by felling him with a well-aimed pellet to the eyeball. Daylight burglars were scarce in West Hampstead in those pre-drug days but we did have plenty of sparrows. I scoured my limited reference library to discover whether these harmless birds were officially considered vermin, thereby falling into the category of legitimate targets according to the BSA advertisement. Delighted to discover in my *I Spy- Birds* the wording under House Sparrow *'considered by farmers to be vermin'* I needed no further authority to load the Airsporter and take up action stations be-hind the ivy. Within moments a small bevy of sparrows landed on and around the chimney pots of the flats to my right. Steady-ing the rifle on the top of the ivy I squeezed off a shot. I missed but the pellet struck a chimney pot and glanced off it with the most satisfying extended *tung* sound of a ricochet as if straight from the sound-track of an old Hopalong film. This had immedi-ate and surprising consequences.

I had failed to notice that on this pleasant summer after-noon the famous writer was enjoying afternoon tea in his pri-vate ground-floor garden with his young wife and their new baby. Being a 'creative' he may have been pre-disposed to over-dramatization as he now leapt to his feet with the cry

"WE'RE BEING SHOT AT! SOMEONE'S SHOOTING AT THE BABY!"

Arms spread wide to shield his wife and new-born he ushered them back into the house, heroically stepping backwards be-hind them until he reached the threshold of the open French doors. Here he stopped and manfully scanned the horizon ob-livious to the danger. No fool, I had dropped to my knees out of sight behind the camouflage ivy. Unfortunately my mother had just finished trimming it that morning and it was no defence against the keen eye of the famous writer who now shouted with full dramatic force

"THERE HE IS! THERE'S A GUNMAN ON THAT BAL-CONY!"

Realising the game was up I got to my feet in full view and retreated into my own house as, with a theatrical gesture, the famous writer pulled shut his double French doors and also disappeared. Once more sensing unwelcome repercussions I re-tired to my bedroom where I lay on the bed reading the latest adventure of *The Wolf of Kabul*.

I hadn't got to the end of it when our front door bell rang and I heard my father leave his study in response. The hallway was adjacent to my bedroom and I could hear deep voices ques-tioning him in urgent tones before the conversation suddenly became convivial. There was a knock on my closed door as my father stuck his head around it saying "Jack I've got two men here who would like to talk to you." I sat up on the bed as he ushered in my visitors with the words "I think we may have cornered the mad gunman!" There stood two large policemen clearly not of the ordinary sort for they wore peaked officer-style hats and had at their waists unconcealed holsters bulging heavily with real pistols. This was all a long time ago so I wasn't in any danger of being unjustly shot. In fact they were smiling a lot while trying to maintain the *gravitas* necessary for delivering a lecture on firearms safety to a ten-year-old. Not sensible in a built up area was the gist of it. They refused my father's offer of a drink saying they were sorry to have intruded but it wasn't every day they received reports of mad gunmen on the loose. They showed me their guns which brought me as close to an orgasmic state as a ten-year-old could get and then pushed me on to new heights of ecstasy by suggesting that in view of the limited opportunities for gun use in West Hampstead would my father and I like to visit the police firing range in Hendon? Having been born into a Jewish family living on Long Island my father had never held a gun in his life until he joined the army just after Pearl Harbour. And then he had quickly swopped it for a typewriter in the Signal Corps. But he couldn't refuse me and as he was always up for a new experience we went to Hendon and had a lovely time. As I said this was all a long time ago when things were done differently.

KEPPEL'S HALL

As the British Empire crumbled away after the war its ability to provide opportunities for graduates of Eton's playing fields vanished with it. Nonetheless the privileged classes continued to despatch their male offspring to boarding schools at a very tender age; a convention that allowed the parents to get on with their lives, happy or sad, unencumbered. In my case having an American father, albeit a liberal-minded one, provided no escape. The difference was that he launched into a search for a co-educational boarding school, a near impossible challenge in England, or probably anywhere, in 1958. Yet he managed it, after a fashion.

Despite my prematurely macho pre-occupation with guns I was a sensitive, insecure child without siblings. My end-of-world scenario arrived the morning I found, face up on my father's desk, a slim brochure announcing '*Keppel's Hall School. A Co-educational Boarding School in Norfolk*'. Above this wording was a black and white photograph of a Dutch-gabled country house. Almost debilitated by nausea I ran sobbing to my mother.

"I can't go to boarding school! You won't let me go will you?"

"Nothing has been decided darling. But you know, it might be more fun than being here at home."
Home was our spacious four-bedroom flat in West Hampstead.

"I won't go! I won't! I won't! Never! I'll die first!"
And so on. I ran to my bedroom, locked the door and collapsed on the bed willing death. Meanwhile in a strategic act of be-

trayal my father was at Keppel's Hall interviewing its headmaster.

As I later heard it this process began with the head pouring three-fingers of Scotch for each of them. Both men loved to drink. My father was a Fleet Street journalist, so alcoholism was almost a qualification. The head was an Irishman who had kissed the Blarney Stone so much the same could be said for him. It was a meeting of Bacchanalian souls. But, unlike my father, the Irishman had a quick temper, with the opportunity to indulge what, on reflection, could only have been a sadistic streak.

The two men became friends and drinking buddies. In later years they often joked about that first meeting when, according to the Irishman, my father's only interrogative question had been 'Do you have any homosexuality in your school?' This he always delivered with a parody of an American drawl. I don't know what answer my dad had been expecting at the time but the 'No' he received was adequate to cement the deal that sealed my fate.

The truth was that Keppel's Hall was hardly more co-ed than any of its competitors. I suspect that in all of them homosexuality, at least amongst some of the boys, was endemic. The headline that had hooked in my father was no more than publicity spin, barely justified by the fact that the resident matron's handicapped daughter sat in on some classes. Further light support for the claim was provided by little Helen, a local pig farmer's daughter who attended classes as a day girl. Not that this privilege was open to any old farmer's daughter. Helen had clout because her father had put up the money to get the place rolling as an independent boarding school. He must have felt that after having spent all that cash to start a private school, there wasn't much point in shelling out more to send his daughter somewhere else. I can see Helen now: small, neat, with dark cropped hair in a green blazer and green checked cotton skirt, a leather satchel over her shoulder. I suppose we must have envied her escaping home every afternoon and weekend but I don't recall we thought about it much because she was never really integral to our world of boarding boys. Such was the school's claim to co-education.

In 1958 Keppel's Hall was in the process of being reborn under the guidance of its new headmaster. In earlier years it had been funded by the London County Council as an institution for the education of boys needing a place of refuge- a sort of cross between school, children's home and borstal. The pig farmer and the Irishman had a vision to forego such public sponsorship and establish a proper independent school catering to the *bourgeoisie*. Whether that vision was focused more by a desire to make money than to educate I couldn't say but when I arrived on April 22nd that year (some dates you don't forget) the transformation had barely got under way.   Dusty grain sacks hung at some of the windows in lieu of curtains and broken, torn furniture littered the common rooms. The cream and green paintwork was scuffed and dirty, but no more so than the malnourished-looking boys in green school jackets, most of whom had just arrived on a train from Bethnal Green.

What on earth had my father been thinking? Looking back I put it down to the egalitarian American approach that often served him well but which sometimes blinded him to those things an Englishman would have sensed a mile away. And to the whisky of course. I was Daniel amongst the lions.

I was allocated a bed in the Long Dorm high in the roof space at the top of a winding narrow staircase originally trodden only by housemaids on the way to their quarters. Despite its name this was the smallest dormitory with half a dozen iron-framed beds, heads to the wall, arranged down each side. This left a narrow passageway from the door to a small window overlooking the Back Lawn. The room was dark with a floor alarmingly on the tilt. On entering a person's natural inclination was to walk toward the light of the window. This would set the wide elm floorboards creaking like a pond full of frogs. I found a crumb of comfort in being told to take one of the two beds by the window until I realised getting to and from it would present a test of bravado. The passageway between the beds was too narrow to permit the passing of two boys simultaneously, its negotiation requiring much giving way. I quickly learnt that courtesy was seen as weakness. In those first days pecking orders had to be established and mettle tested.

Part of my survival kit, the mainstay of it, possibly the whole of it, was a photograph of my mother. At this point in her life she had become quite glamorous with bounteous blonde hair and a beauty spot. Good-looking and high-spirited she was naturally equipped with plentiful *joie de vivre*: a working class country girl who, due to the opportunities thrown up by the war, had married into a wealthy New York family. She had taken to her new life as a duck to water. Evidence of this new life was well represented by some black and white studio portraits taken by a professional London photographer who had executed them after the style of Marilyn Monroe, then at the height of her fame. It was one of these photos, a head and (bare) shoulders shot nicely mounted in a leather folder that I tucked under my pillow that first night at boarding school.

What I had failed to anticipate, and no one had warned me, was that in an established start-of-term ritual the bigger bully boys from the dorm on the floor below would raid us underlings at lights out to both establish their authority and seize whatever plunder they might find. They were delighted with my photograph. A big lad called Bunthoyd made off with it, calling to his mates to come and 'have a butcher's' while making whatever lascivious comments were used by schoolboys in the 1950s. This was sufficiently distressing for me to report the theft to the headmaster's wife at breakfast the next morning. This lady, in an entirely unofficial capacity, provided the school's only resource for the support of those suffering emotional trauma. It was a decidedly risky action to take on my part for by then I had already sensed that 'squitting' on schoolmates was unpardonable and could result in permanent ostracism, not to mention nasty physical reprisals from those squitted on. That afternoon I found the leather photograph wallet lying back on my bed intact. There were no further repercussions. I think that was because even amongst the heathen brotherhood of schoolboys besmirching someone's mother was seen as a little beyond the Pale. After all, in that regard we were all vulnerable.

Teatime that first day came as a surprise for a rich kid from Hampstead. In 1958 strawberry jam, at least the institutional-quality stuff supplied to the school, came in unmarked 7lb tins. It was still made to a wartime recipe from mashed turnips, food colouring and sugar syrup. It spooned out a translucent crimson. We spread it thinly over pale margarine made from whale oil. This we scraped over sliced white bread that would soon be manufactured by the newly industrialised Chorleywood process. It was the fill-gut of our schooldays.

Rationing- the whole idea of not having as much to eat as you wanted- also caught me unawares. The allocated amount of jam, margarine and bread was placed on each table before we entered the dining hall. There was no replenishment. As I knifed a large blob of margarine from its pot at that first teatime my equilibrium was shaken by a bellowed rebuke from the table prefect.

"That has to serve all of us you know- put some back!"
The grey shadow of the war was receding only slowly from the tables of state-sponsored boarding schools.

Grisly stews, black potatoes and lumpy custard all figured largely in this new and novel diet but I recall being particularly horrified by the dense grey filling of the meat pies that were sliced up into portions for our lunch on two days each week.

"What is this meat?" I asked the boy next to me.

"Mole," he answered without hesitation "mole pie. You've seen Lenny with his traps on the Back Lawn" (Lenny was the school gardener).

I stopped masticating.

"Well, there you are then."

The weekly letter I was allowed to write home conveyed this information to my mother as reinforcement to my usual pleas to be repatriated to Hampstead. I never did learn what the grey stuff really was.

Actually the mole idea was not entirely incredible because Lenny did contribute more to our diet than vegetables from the walled garden. Enraged by the despoiling of his Brussel sprouts by wood pigeons, he started shooting them and later presented the cook with a wheelbarrow full of feathered corpses. She instructed him to pluck them after which they were roasted and served to us for Sunday lunch, a whole bird each. Tearing apart the carcases with greasy fingers we thought it a tremendous feast and a huge improvement over our normal fare. After that we were always urging Lenny to take up his gun again.

In fact I was fast learning how to survive. There had been the initial shock, the theft of the photograph, the new discipline, the awful food and the torture sessions for new boys. The latter involved a group of older boys ambushing a victim on the Back Lawn and dragging him out of sight into the surrounding woods. Here he would be given Chinese wrist burns or have prickly grass stems threaded through his hair and yanked free. This would remove small clumps of hair by the roots. Or have the back of his hand burnt with a magnifying glass. Or be debagged and thrown into the nettles, or all of these things one after the other. If you could come through this trial without bawling or later squitting you would achieve some measure of respect and be left alone. Thus the beginning of the time-honoured route by which English public schoolboys grow into men of stiff upper lip and repressed emotion. Some boys didn't make it. There were those who through nature or nurture were not inherently strong mentally. There was Pooley, a great pasty, slab-faced lad already six-foot in his early teens. It was the fate of Pooley that has stayed with me.

Ironically, given my father's one original question to the head, the school was rife with homosexuality. As boys entered puberty hormones were released which could not be denied. Masturbation, and occasionally mutual experimentation, took root. A succession of masters, attracted to minor boarding schools by this scenario, exploited it. In recent times many of these chickens have come home to roost with allegations of historical abuse, but in those days they had free range. Keppel's Hall was no exception. Pooley may have been truly gay or simply overwhelmed by his hormones but in any event due to a malicious tip-off he was caught by the headmaster in a toilet cubicle with a younger boy. Despite the gross injustice, given our knowledge of the adventures of one or other paedophile master, we knew this offence rated a public beating. The headmaster was fond of the cane, so much so that he would occasionally hide behind an open door to observe an approaching boy through the gap between the hinges. If the boy's coat, say, was not zipped the regulation two-thirds of the way up the head would let the miscreant pass before leaping out and whacking the cane across the back of the boy's bare legs with maximum force.

In contrast to such surprise attacks the morning of a public beating would see boys and masters summoned to assemble in the gymnasium. In recognition of female sensitivities Matron, Carol her daughter and Helen were excluded. The atmosphere would be tense and fearful, for no boy could be quite sure that he was not to be the victim of the headmaster's wrath. The imminent witnessing of an obscenity engendered an awful silence. Perhaps someone might whisper a guess as to the identity of the accused. Summary executions in Japanese prison camps must have felt much the same. After several minutes of this tension the headmaster would make a brisk and theatrical entry through the swing doors to deliver a brief speech outlining the nature of the crime and the punishment he had decided it deserved. This was usually six, occasionally twelve, strokes of the cane depending on his mood. Most of us would then breathe easy at the realisation the crime could not be ours. Not so for the guilty party for whom this might be the first indication of his sentence, though the calling of an impromptu assembly might well have suggested it. The head would name the now quivering boy, ordering him to the changing rooms to put on his PT shorts. There was no provision for appeal.

Weak-kneed, Pooley had to be escorted out to the changing rooms by the assistant headmaster and dragged back sobbing. The headmaster had meanwhile left to fetch his cane from his office. He reappeared through the swing doors flexing it between his hands, clearly angered by Pooley's lack of moral fibre. He ordered Pooley to bend. The first stroke, delivered with venom shocking to see, straightened the boy up and set him running. The head bellowed in rage for him to stand still before giving in to pursuit, black gown flying behind him as if he were some vengeful Satanic angel while he aimed wild strokes at whatever part of Pooley's anatomy came within reach. Lanks of grey hair discomposed themselves from around his balding pate. Spittle flecked his gown. The bawling Pooley desperately attempted to escape by burrowing his way behind the ranks of watching boys. Some of these were jumping aside to avoid the flailing cane. Eventually the exhausted head gave up the chase. Red-faced and breathing heavily he stalked out angrily, only too aware he had absolutely lost it in front of a disapproving audience. We filed away to our classes leaving a destroyed Pooley on his knees, his arms and legs covered in red welts. I think many of us were just as scarred, if not so plainly. Pooley left the school shortly after this.

The regime of severe discipline and harsh living conditions occasionally persuaded a boy to take destiny into his own hands by making a break for freedom. Escape back to life on easy-street at home in London seemed an enticing goal. Of course as boys in the '50s we were immersed in dramatic stories of wartime breakouts from prison camps. The resonance of those narratives with our own situation was loud, with the result that any boy who absconded immediately gained respect as a heroic figure. The discovery of an empty bed when we first woke in the morning would send a *frisson* of fear and excitement through the school as the whisper flashed through the dorms: 'So-and-so's gone, scarpered!' This was not least because, in terms of brutality of punishment, attempted escape ranked with being caught *inflagrante* in a homosexual act. Certainly neither crime would enhance the re-born school's reputation if brought to public attention. The head was determined to stamp on both.

On the day of an escape attempt our whole routine would be disrupted as the headmaster, members of staff and even the local police would set out to co-ordinate a recapture. The standard procedure was for a master to watchfully drive the local lanes while someone else, usually the police, staked out the nearest railway station. Rumours would fly around the classrooms all morning:

'He's made it- he's in London.'

'He's in Norwich.'

'They've got him!'

'They can't find him.'

'The police have got him locked up.'

We were always crest-fallen with a sense of vicarious disappointment when, usually by lunchtime, a car containing the bedraggled escapee and a triumphant looking head would be observed crunching up the gravel of the Long Drive. The car was always driven slowly so as to impress the futility of attempting to escape on the maximum number of observers. The miscreant would be locked in solitary confinement in the sick room overnight but next day, after punishment had been executed, we would cluster around the hero to hear his stories of platoons of policemen pursuing across ploughed fields, of hiding in hollow trees and of thumbing lifts in gigantic lorries.

A short, bony boy called Greaves made repeated attempts

to get away. He lived with us in the Long Dorm that first term and very early one spring morning climbed down the drainpipe from the window. On that occasion he apparently made it as far as the railway station in Diss, which we thought tremendously impressive. Obviously we all spent hours discussing theories of escape and the best techniques of evasion but as I remember it nobody ever got as far as London or home. Most had not the nerve for the attempt. Despite the repeated thrashings I think it was the lust for glory that motivated Greaves and finally resulted in his permanent expulsion. Perhaps that was his plan all along, but it had involved a good deal of pain.

After my first year an older boy called Patchett became my best friend due to a shared love of fishing. Patchett was in the form above me. Whenever our free time coincided on a Saturday or Sunday afternoon we would seek permission to walk to the nearby gravel pits to fish for little perch and rudd. We might have bicycled there except Patchett wasn't allowed to ride a bike because he very occasionally suffered temporary blackouts which would result in his stopping whatever he was doing to gaze about blankly for the ten to twenty seconds it took before his normal senses returned. It meant he sometimes missed seeing a bite when we were fishing but the bigger problem came when he played as goalie for the Under 13s team. In school we were of course all aware of Patchett's problem and would discount any goals scored when he was suffering a blackout. The more difficult issue arose in inter-school games when the opposing side would be discreetly advised of the situation and requested not to press home an attack if Patchett was observed to be 'out of it'. As Patchett's blackouts were normally induced by excitement this was not a very sustainable arrangement and was in any event subject to the suspicion of abuse. Patchett was soon replaced as goalie.

More serious from my own point of view was that the

headmaster had observed our friendship and had subsequently decided to advise the older boy to spend more time in associations within his own peer group and less time with members of the junior classes, in other words me. In the less than subtle manner of schoolboys Patchett notified me of his receipt of this advice accompanied by the declaration that regrettably our friendship would have to be terminated. This did nothing for my self-esteem nor for my opinion of the headmaster

Nevertheless fours years after starting at boarding school I had managed to come through the trauma and pain, had escaped any sexual exploitation and felt reasonably comfortable as I started, well ahead of time, a programme of 'O' level GCE exams. I was fourteen. It was at this point, in the spring of 1962, that my father once more masterminded a tectonic shift in my education. He decided, as he put it to his mate the headmaster, 'the boy needs to have some American influence'. I was sent to a school on a cattle ranch in northern Arizona.

SUNDAY MORNING

Four men sit around a garden table on the patio of a ranch-style bungalow, newly built on the inland edge of the coastal town of Aldeburgh. It is a cloudless morning in June 1962. The table is loaded with brown bottles of pale ale, yellow cans of Pilsner lager, a bottle of Wild Turkey bourbon, another of scotch and numerous glasses. Ed, an American in an open-necked red tartan shirt, is the owner of the bungalow. The other three men are his hunch-backed gardener Bill Bloomfield, the local wine merchant 'Toasty' Baggott, and Stanley from the brick works located on the edge of the marshes just over the road. Ed is nearing fifty, the others are at least a decade older.

Beyond the open French doors that lead onto the patio Ed's wife Hilda is rattling pans in the red and white open-plan kitchen as she readies the Sunday lunch. Every few minutes she punctuates these preparations by walking over to the threshold to stand in the sunshine and join in the men's banter. They are having a good time and Hilda is an integral part of the occasion. She is a vivacious blonde with Marilyn Monroe figure and a quick laugh that shows pearl-white teeth behind scarlet lips. Her hands are protected by yellow washing up gloves. In one she holds a potato peeler; in the other, slightly incongruous, a tall tumbler of scotch on the rocks that she raises to her lips, leaving crescents of red on its rim. She steps out onto the patio to put glass and peeler on the table, pulls off the gloves and takes a lit cigarette from her husband's hand. The men pour more drinks.

These Sunday morning get-togethers at Ed's place are something of a routine for the five people present. Ed is a journalist, an editor, on the North American desk of a news agency with its head office on Fleet Street. During the week he stays in a small flat off Fetter Lane. On Friday afternoons, rubbing shoulders with a handful of City professionals for whom East Suffolk is also home, he catches the train from Liverpool Street to Saxmundham, changes onto the Aldeburgh branch line and finally walks the quarter-mile up the hill to Hilda and this bungalow they had built in 1960 in a sort of *faux* Californian style.

As nails are to carpenters so drink is to journalists, making Ed one of Toasty's more significant clients and qualifying him for Sunday morning home deliveries. On the first occasion the wine merchant's van pulled up on the gravel in front of the new bungalow Ed, smiling from ear to ear, had thrown open the front door with a 'Hey Buddy we been waitin' for ya. Come on in! Wad-er-ya drink?' This was not the sort of greeting Toasty was accustomed to at the back doors of Aldeburgh's moneyed classes who usually dismissed him with a perfunctory 'Thank you very much'. But Toasty was a man who loved the stuff of his trade so, after stacking assorted cartons of wine, beer and spirits on the kitchen floor, he accepted a glass of Tolly IPA. Toasty had acquired his name from his tendency to compose rambling toasts celebrating even the most insignificant of occasions. The induction of a new 'international' client clearly deserved recognition so the wine merchant now raised his glass to Ed, to Anglo-American friendship and to Ed's long and happy life in the new house: a prospect, he added, only existing due to America's support in the war and even possibly to Ed's personal contribution to it. He then settled himself with his glass into one of Hilda's unconventionally modern leopard-print easy chairs. Ed loved this sort of comradely banter and immediately warmed to Toasty. In the course of the subsequent conversation Toasty recommended Bill, his mate and drinking companion at The Victoria on the High Street, as gardener for the newly laid out lawns and flowerbeds around the bungalow. A week or two after that Bill recommended Stanley, another regular at the Vic, as an excellent handyman in his spare time and so, given

Ed's disregard for the conventions of the English class system, a very egalitarian sort of drinking club coalesced around Toasty's weekly delivery.

These boozy Sunday mornings are famously jocular occasions for Ed and Hilda are relaxed and generous hosts. Nor are they suspect newcomers. Ed had spent the war years in a Nissen hut on the nearby fighter base at Leiston and had met Hilda in The Volunteer one Saturday night in March 1944. She had been a domestic in service to a family well known in the district with a big house overlooking the sea where Hilda, a cut above the average, had acted as nanny, sometime cook and general *aide-de-camp*. The shared hardship of the war is the background generating an empathy amongst this group, now prospering in the new affluence of the 'You've never had it so good' Macmillan years.

The men have their tubular metal garden chairs pushed back. They lean forward to fill their glasses or to take cigarettes from the open packs on the table: flip-top Kensitas and the soft, blocky packets of Lucky Strike obtained from the American base at Bentwaters- now home to Cold War jets and nuclear missiles. They lean back again to drink and to draw on the cigarettes. The wit is quick; the laughter pauses only to allow the next quip. The sun and the camaraderie are warm, Hilda is gorgeous in the kitchen and the men don't mind if things never get any better than this.

Ed sticks his cigarette between his lips and reaches forward to refill his glass with lager. Squinting through the smoke he misjudges and the beer rises foaming over the rim of the slim glass to drip through the slats of the table, threatening shoes and trousers with a wetting. The men all sit up sharply, pulling their feet under the chairs as if a snake had just dropped onto the table. Ed calls to the kitchen

"Honey, bring a cloth- I'm having a little accident"
Hilda appears and wipes the beer from the table as the men move bottles and glasses and wet cigarette packets aside. She then makes great show of wiping Ed's lap with an admonishing

"Have you wet yourself again darling?"

She then straightens and turns to the others.

"Any of you lot need cleaning up too?" she asks with an air of mock efficiency. Stanley raises both his arms to expose his lap.

"Yes I seems a little damp down here Hilda," he says hopefully.

"Yes well I'm not that wet behind the ears you old lecher" Hilda grins at him.

"Randy old Yanks allus did git the best wimmin!" retorts Stanley.

They all laugh as Hilda disappears back to the kitchen.

From under a glass ashtray crammed with cigarette butts Ed has withdrawn a lager-soaked sheet of blue paper printed on both sides. It is a list and entry form for the various classes of competition in the annual horticultural show held at his news agency. For a city-based operation a surprising number of the employees are keen gardeners, and a great deal of kudos attaches to winning.

Ed is holding the sheet between thumb and forefinger of both hands.

"Well boys, are we gonna wipe the board this year- show those city slickers what we can do down here?"

"Yew wanta be wipin' that bit o' paper fust" says Stanley. The show is to be held in a week's time on a Monday to allow competitors to bring their entries in fresh from the weekend. Ed is a keen participant but there is a difficulty this year. The soil of the bungalow garden is poor sand as yet unimproved by mulching and composts and the season to date has been unusually dry: flowers and vegetables are small or withered and are not the stuff of exhibitions. But Ed is an optimistic American. He reads from the entry form.

"'Plate of 3 Broad Beans in Pod' Well, the beans are pretty good Bill?"

"Be past it by next week" growls Bill sitting forward on his chair with his elbows on the edge of the table, a posture which stretches the frayed hand-me-down suit jacket across his back, accentuating its hump.

"You passed it years ago mate" offers Toasty "but you're still here."

"Yeah but he hint nevva won nawfen either" adds Stanley.

"Nor will he, less it's for misery" says Toasty "take bloody gold at the Olympics for that, the old sod. Don't you take no notice of him Eddy; you put yer beans in if you want to. Faint heart never won a fair lady."

"'Two Lettuces'" reads Ed "they're not too bad Bill, sprinkler was on them all last night."

"*Two* lettuces" scowls Bill "you on't have one lettuce not shot by next week, not in this heat."

"There 'e goo agin" says Stanley "Mr. Sunshine!"
Hilda has come back to the French doors, glass in hand.

"Oh stop picking on poor old Bill," she says through falsely pouting red lips. She steps out onto the patio and bends down to put a bare arm around Bill's shoulders.

"He just doesn't want you to be disappointed Ed. That's it, isn't it Bill- you're just trying to be kind?"

"Now that *would* definitely get him a medal" chuckles Toasty "for Outstanding Improvement!"
They all laugh except Bill who has nonetheless brightened slightly under Hilda's pantomime protection.

"Could try the gladioli," he suggests, looking over to Ed.

"But we don't have any gladioli," says Ed "do we?"

"You mightn't," says Bill "but I have. Bloody good 'uns. Don't reckon anyone could touch 'em."

It's general knowledge that Bill neither owns nor rents property but lives in a glorified shed at the end of a garden in Park Road that belongs to the solicitor whose erstwhile jacket he is wearing. In lieu of rent he looks after the solicitor's garden. Money for food and beer (the latter the larger proportion) he obtains by working as a jobbing gardener at several of the other large properties spaced along Park Road. It is clear what he has in mind. Ed is taken aback.

"You can't do that, the whole idea is that you grow your

own entry."

"That may be the idea" counters Bill "but if you hint got the stuff what are you s'posed to do?"

"Not enter" Ed says huffily and suddenly a nasty thought occurs to him.

"Those peas I won runner up with last year- were they mine, or were they stolen from some other customer of yours?" Bill looks down at the table, picks up his beer, takes a double swallow and puts the glass down as he catches Ed's now angry stare.

"Well, since you ask, them peas was Dr Turner's. Yours was full o' maggots."

A sense of embarrassment has silenced the other two men. Ed is genuinely shocked. For all his maturity, the war years and a career in the Fleet Street jungle he retains a naïve belief in American-style small-town decency. At least in such matters as cheating with your, or somebody else's, vegetables. Hilda is still standing beside Bill. She wades in.

"Oh for heaven's sake, what difference does it make whose bloody peas or gladioli they are? It's only meant to be a bit of fun!"
Another bulb flashes in Ed's memory.

"Honey, you won a first for the tastiest strawberry jam. I guess that started out at the Co-op grocery store."

"Don't be silly sweetie, that was *Wilkins'* best 'Little Scarlet'" laughs Hilda looking sideways towards Toasty and Stanley, winking at each in turn. Ed stands up,

"Jeez, I don't believe it. You guys 're all a bunch of immoral crooks" he announces and stomps off through the French doors to the bathroom, leaving the others wondering whether he's genuinely angry or playfully teasing. The booze makes it difficult to tell.

Hilda sits down in the vacated chair, sips her scotch, takes a puff of cigarette and, tilting her head back, languidly blows smoke towards the blue sky,

"Well, it isn't serious, is it" This more statement than

question. "I bet the others all do it."

The men are wary of taking sides, unsure of where their loyalties should lie. Stanley seeks to defuse the tension,

"That hully smell nice whatever yer cookin in there Hilda."

Hilda is a fine cook, a legacy of her time in service.

"Nice leg of lamb from Salter's" she replies, "with plenty of garlic and your rosemary out of the garden Bill. Stay and have some. Why don't you all stay, it's a big leg. I'll put some more spuds in?"

The three men smile but all know this would be a step too far under the circumstances. Stanley answers for them.

"That'ud be very nice Hilda but I dun reckon I cud goo hoom artawud. Winnie ud kill me. More 'n likely she's got the dumplins in now."

Ed has reappeared in the doorway. His face makes it clear the alcohol is pushing him further towards irritation rather than back to his earlier geniality. Hilda makes no move to get up. Making their excuses the three guests get to their feet and replace their chairs neatly back at the table, leaving Hilda marooned like an exposed salient. Toasty will give Stanley a lift home in his van. Bill is bent over fastening cycle clips: his old bicycle with a wicker basket attached to the handlebars leans against the stake of a newly planted tree on the lawn. He pulls it upright and pushes past the edge of the patio towards the driveway. Looking across at Ed he asks

"What do you want to do about next week then Eddy?"

Ed's reply is peevish.

"I think we'll have to leave it this year Bill, if you think our stuff's not good enough." Then unable to repress a surfacing of self-righteousness he adds

"I don't think I should cheat on my colleagues."

He stays standing proprietarily in the doorway. Wordlessly Bill mounts his bike and, with difficulty in the loose gravel, wobbles off down the drive behind Toasty's departing van. The lamb is delicious but is unable to rescue the lunch. Ed is obsessed with the cheating issue.

"Darling, I was brought up never to lie, cheat or steal. George Washington and the cherry tree, all that stuff. At home, school, even in the Air Force, damn it! You just didn't do it. It's a matter of respect. What if we brought up Jack with the idea it's OK to cheat? He'd be expelled. That could mark him for life! Then would you think cheating's OK?"

"Oh Ed, let it go for God's sake. It's only a flower show." Hilda puts forward her earlier defence.

"I bet you nobody else worries. What about your Canadian friend Ferguson? He got Best All Round Vegetables last year and he can't even grow a dish of cress in that pokey flat of his. Remember he laughed about it when we had dinner there? It had all shrivelled up and died."

"No Hilda, it *was* his stuff- his mother's got a big place down in Kent."

"Well then? With a gardener?"

Ed pauses to consider his position. Topped up by lunchtime wine the morning's alcohol is fomenting irritability to anger.

"Yes maybe, but that's not the same thing. At least it's his own family, not some strange doctor on Park Road. Anyway buying strawberry jam and putting it in a plain jar is a bit much. Wouldn't you say?"

These last words are spoken aggressively with a nasty parody of English accent, Ed's head and chin pushed forward, a demeanour that sets Hilda seething. She spits out her words in carefully enunciated English.

"No. I wouldn't say. As a matter of fact. But what I would say is it's not half as bad as the cheating some people get up to!" Hilda holds his eyes, refusing to let go. The lamb turns in Ed's stomach making him feel nauseous. He puts down his fork and continues to stare at her

"And what do you mean by that?"

"I'll let you work that out."

Hilda drops her eyes, rises from her chair and begins noisily clearing the plates. Ed stands. He can't answer. He pushes in his chair. It's a small town, people talk. Valerie was on the train on Friday as usual. She will be there tonight. He looks forward to their journeys together. He can't deny it to himself and he has the sense to know that it is pointless now to deny it to Hilda. He is defeated, humbled, the hangover already beginning. He caves in, managing a self-pitying 'Thank you for lunch' in the manner of a small boy admonished. He shuffles away towards the study in the spare bedroom.

A few minutes later he comes silently back to the kitchen where Hilda is at the sink washing up with her back to him. She is staring pointedly out into the brightness of the garden. Without speaking he approaches her and moves to wrap his arms around her waist from behind. With a flurry of soapsuds and yellow gloves she pushes his arms away. Wordlessly he retreats again, this time to the bedroom to pack his bag for town. The shouting will come soon enough.

Down at 'The Vic' Bill is leaning against the bar, his chin glumly propped in one hand beside a half-drunk pint. He has been joined by Toasty who, against the odds, has managed to drop off Stanley and make his final two deliveries without putting any more dents in his well-scraped van.

"Well what do you reckon bor?" he asks Bill.
Bill doesn't bother to lift his chin from his hand.

"What I reckon ole mate is we might be in here a bit earlier next Sunday."

"Well, I int gonna drink to that" says Toasty.

AMERICAN PIE

T he Salt River valley in southern Arizona is hot. Summer days often hit 40 degrees Celsius or even more. Annual rainfall is only about 7 inches, so even with irrigation from the river, which sometimes dries to a trickle, it has always been a tough place to farm. Which is why, in 1929, a family of pioneers sold their dairy farm in the valley and moved seventy-five miles north to become beef cattle ranchers in higher, cooler country near the little settlement of Mayer.

His name was Charles 'Chick' Orme and hers was Minna. Moving posed a problem for their three young children. Down in the valley they had been close to the fast-growing city of Phoenix with shops and schools but further north there were few people and fewer facilities. The nearest school was in Prescott, forty miles away over dirt roads. The solution was to hire a teacher to live in on the ranch to educate the Orme children and those of the hired hands who worked the cows. Soon neighbouring ranchers were asking if their children could avoid the long haul to Prescott by joining the little group at the Orme ranch. A school was born.

Chick and Minna were both Stanford university graduates so they new a bit about education. They set high standards and the school prospered. When in 1945 Charles Junior also graduated from Stanford he decided to take on this minor educational venture and develop it as a college preparatory boarding school with himself as headmaster. By the time I got there in 1962 it was becoming known. Clearly a school on a cattle ranch in the middle of nowhere was unique and by nature exclusive. But it wasn't *that* far from L.A. and California. It was attracting some big names. Jimmy Stewart's stepson went there. Ronnie Reagan sent his daughter Patti. The scions of some of the nation's biggest and most famous companies appeared.

Part of the attraction was that the place continued as a working cattle ranch. Known as the Quarter Circle V Bar, with a matching brand, it spread over 40,000 acres of federal and private range. This was big, wild country full of pronghorn antelope and occasional mountain lions. The school though was small and intimate, contained within a resident community of fewer than two hundred people altogether, including ranch hands, teaching staff and students. It was run, as its literature liked to emphasise, as a big family. Chick was 'Uncle' Chick, his wife was 'Aunt' Minna, the headmaster was 'Charlie' and all the rest of the staff were known by their first names. It presented the epitome of wholesome Western American living.

On arrival every new student was assigned a horse and taught how to ride it. Each student was also assigned a daily chore: feeding the hogs or the turkeys, taking the horses back out to pasture, emptying trash cans or cleaning classrooms. Twice a year there was a round-up of the cattle. Anyone who wanted could tag along on horseback. Once a year the whole school packed itself into trucks for a two-week camping trip up to Utah or Colorado or down into Mexico.

In between times there was weekend camping. Find a willing adult to come along and one or more of you could ride your horse as far as you wanted on the Saturday, camp overnight and ride back on the Sunday. In that arid landscape we would head for the lines of big cottonwood poplars that signalled the presence of creek beds. Here, where the water came to the surface in clear shaded pools, fish darted away from your approach and turtles plopped from sunning on rocky ledges. In the spring hummingbirds hovered over drifts of wild flowers and the cottonwoods filled with chattering flocks of small birds.

Sometimes we could persuade Beanie the horse wrangler

to chaperone a ride. Beanie was a wiry little guy with a face sunburnt the colour of red ochre under a ten-gallon hat. When he removed the hat, which was normally only at the last moment before sleeping, a shockingly white bald pate was revealed. Beanie was a favourite because around the campfire he would entertain us with wildly apocryphal stories about the bad old days in Arizona. Then he would take up his battered guitar and sing cowboy numbers like the 'Streets of Laredo' and 'Cool Water'. Those well-worn favourites took on new life when delivered by an old cowhand accompanied by coyotes yapping under a western sky ablaze with stars. Tired and saddle-sore we would listen as we stared into the flames, stirring the sand at our feet with twigs and waving the mesquite smoke out of our eyes. Once we were shaken out of our somnolence by the scream of a mountain lion in the darkness not very far away.

"Jesus, what the hell was ... ?"
Beanie hardly missed a beat:

"Just some ole lion feelin' lonely. He won't bother us."
Nevertheless we moved our sleeping bags as near to the fire as we could get and Beanie moved the horses in closer to the camp. Norfolk it was not.

The alternative for a Saturday was a town trip to Prescott. Prescott sits in the foothills of the Bradshaw mountains at 5000' of elevation in a rugged landscape of pine and juniper, the sort of landscape people might imagine if you were talking about, say, Colorado instead of Arizona. Not a saguaro cactus in sight. Those are the iconic trident-shaped exclamations that punctuate the hot sands of the Sonoran desert in the lower third of the state. Two thirds of Arizona's population live down there around Phoenix and Tucson. Back in the early 60s this left the upper two thirds of the state very empty, a country of cattle ranches, homesteads and abandoned mining towns. We enjoyed a lot of space. Camping out in it was fun but for teenagers cloistered on a remote ranch the lure of the town was usually irresistible.

Prescott embodied the essence of a small pioneer town. Until 1889 it served as capital of the Arizona territory. It was said Wyatt Earp's brother Virgil had lived there. In the central square a white porticoed courthouse stood grandly under tall shade trees. At its front a flagpole supported a large 'Stars and Stripes', ceremoniously raised and lowered at the beginning and end of each day. Around the periphery of this square an old fashioned boardwalk fronted timber-built stores, restaurants and saloons. There was a bank or two, some real estate offices, a barbershop, a movie house and even, in 1962, a corner soda fountain: that strangely American marriage of pharmacy and milk bar. Small-town America.

Old station wagons and dusty pickup trucks with ranch dogs asleep in the back lined the street. Sometimes there was even a horse with the reins looped over a hitching rail. The men, and a lot of the women, dressed in Levis and pearl-buttoned western shirts. They wore wide-brimmed cowboy hats and tooled leather boots that clack-clacked loudly along the echoey boardwalks. Occasionally a cowboy straight from the range would still have on leather chaps and spurs that jangled metallically on the boards. The feed store and the sporting goods store were the busiest, the former selling all farm and ranch requisites, the latter guns and ammunition. One side of the square was known as 'Whisky Row' with a swing-door saloon called 'The Palace' that claimed to be the oldest saloon in Arizona. There was a gift shop and a gallery selling Western art but the tide of tourism had yet to corrupt the town's original function as a service centre for the region's working community. We teenagers would sit on chromed swivel stools at the counter of one of the diners. We ordered cheeseburgers and Nesselrode pie and drank root beer or Dr Pepper's. Afterwards we would browse the stores before ending up in the movie house to watch films starring Gregory Peck or John Wayne.

◆ ◆ ◆

What on earth was I doing in Arizona living and eating American pie? Physically, culturally and educationally I was a very, very long way from Norfolk and Keppel's Hall (not to mention my parents). In matters of discipline, dress, food and relationships with the staff Orme was about as far as you could get in the opposite direction.

On my first day I was allocated a 'buddy' to act as guide and mentor. Passing through the school's main open space- 'the barnyard'- we came across a tall man in jeans, checked shirt and Stetson hat.

"This is the headmaster Charlie," said my buddy,

"Charlie, this is Jack from England."

Charlie held out his hand to me and drawled

"Well, howdy Jack, welcome to Orme."

Conditioned to punishment for the least hint of insouciance in front of my English headmaster I snapped to attention like an S.S. officer and said

"Thank you Mr.Orme, sir!"

Charlie smiled back.

"Most folk around here just call me Charlie- that okay with you?"

"Yes, yes of course sir" I stuttered.

Charlie kept smiling and walked on leaving me flustered. This was all very new.

A little further into our tour of the campus I spotted a brick-built drinking fountain installed on a footpath between classrooms.

"Who is that for?" I asked my mentor.

He looked puzzled.

"Anyone of course, anyone who's thirsty."

"You mean us, the students?" I said.

"Of course!"

I could hardly believe it. In Norfolk had such a thing existed I knew its use would be restricted as a privilege for teachers or prefects, an opportunity to impose another small humiliation on ordinary boys. It was an absolute revelation.

The explanation of my presence in this new world was that my father, although born on Long Island, had, in the 1930s, been enrolled at the University of Arizona in Tucson. Initially he had attended Yale but after his first year the doctors had told him he probably had TB. My grandparents had therefore sent him west to the dry air of Arizona. That was the connection. That and the fact that Charlie Orme was another headmaster who enjoyed his whisky. He too became a lifelong friend of my father's. There was definitely a pattern. Then there was the important point that the Orme School was *truly* co-educational. With no paedophiles. They probably didn't know the word. After all northern Arizona was in the redneck, homophobic American West, the country Annie Proulx writes about in *Brokeback Mountain*. Having said that, the school, through its students, had close ties with the San Francisco Bay Area, and Phoenix was becoming more cosmopolitan year on year. Despite the location our outlook was decidedly liberal.

The co-education became more important as we advanced through the grades and hormone surges intensified. Generally speaking we fell into one or other of two groups: the surfers from the beaches of southern California or the cowboys from Arizona. Of course not everyone was from southern California or Arizona so the 'wannabees' picked one group or the other to follow, although there were a few independents- geeks and the like. The surfers tended to play sports while the cowboys rode horses, practised for rodeos and raised calves.

The surfers definitely had the best girls, blonde and tanned, although some of the cowgirls had quite a following: something erotic about being up there on horseback, legs splayed. But inevitably the surfers were miles ahead on 'cool'. The Beach Boys were making a huge impact with *Surfin' Safari*, *Surfin' USA* and *Little Deuce Coupe*. Everybody was singing 'let's go surfin' now, everybody's learnin' how, come on and

safari with me'. The cowboys only had Johnny Cash and Lor-
etta Lynn. I was in the useful position of being able to slip in
and out of both camps with the *passé-partout* of being British
and thereby beyond any meaningful geographical demarcation.
Until of course the Beatles arrived with a bang, London became
swinging and, with absolutely no justification at all, I became
cool. I was even made captain of an embryonic soccer team on
the basis that I might understand the offside rule (we lost every
inter-school game).

Being British with a funny voice did help with the girls
though, to the extent that when we got to the weeks before the
Junior-Senior Prom I was able to invite and, more importantly,
be accepted by Patti Reagan. She was in the year below me, a
slim, olive-skinned girl with straight black hair and prominent
dental braces. Despite the metalwork she was a good-looking
catch so it was something of a coup to get her. Actually I think
her friends orchestrated the whole thing in the belief, completely off the mark in my case, that having a Brit for a date had
to be super-cool. I suppose I was seventeen so Patti must have
been fifteen or sixteen. Her father had just launched a campaign
to become governor of California.

The prom venue was a new restaurant in Phoenix called
'The Beefeaters', themed, in accord with the times, on all things
British. To get there we had to bus the seventy-five miles down
the Black Canyon highway after first presenting our dates with
elaborate corsages of lilies. A short avenue of gas-fired flares
led to the restaurant's entrance, these intended to create an
Elizabethan ambience while adding a few more degrees to the
hot desert night. The *double-entendre* of the restaurant's name
was supported by two sweating doormen got up in theatrical
outfits copied from the Tower. Each held a plastic pikestaff and
stood on either side of the entrance trying to maintain poses ap-
proximating to the motionless discipline associated with the
Queen's bodyguards. Our dates were resplendent in shiny silk
or rich velvet, decorated with the corsages we had given them,
while we escorts were kitted out in tuxedos. Mine was white.

A passer-by might have mistaken the scene for a pantomime, which I suppose it was. The meal was of course beef and, although we were chaperoned, someone had managed to smuggle in beer disguised in brown paper bags in traditional Prohibition style.

A live band played the latest Rolling Stones releases. This gave us a good deal of satisfaction as the Stones were perceived as the bad boys of British pop relative to the Beatles, so a touch more *frisson* was added to our evening. We jiggled around the dance floor shouting along with the lyrics of '*this will be the last time*' and '*hey you get off of ma cloud*', while the more extrovert girls competed to display the uninhibited moves they had studied on news reports coming from Swinging London. Dancing was not the end of the evening's planned entertainment however as after an hour or so of sweaty gyrations and surreptitious swigging of beer we re-boarded the bus to be transported to a fairground where a number of adrenalin-inducing rides were operating. These were my undoing.

The one that actually got me was the thing that looks like a giant windmill with a rotating capsule at each end of a huge single arm. This arm, or sail, goes round and round in a vertical plane, first clockwise then anti-clockwise, while the capsules containing the punters rotate at 90 degrees to the arm, first one way, then the other. Intoxication or youth are pre-requisites to the mistake of getting on it and I had both. My digestive system indicated it was in trouble as soon as the machine began operation but it was too late to get off. Patti and I were securely strapped in side by side as we were hoisted toward the stars in an upside down position. The committee of senior students that had contributed to the planning of our evening may have been working on the theory that if you could scare your girl sufficiently she would be putty in your hands afterwards. That certainly wasn't working for me as all I could think about was the gravitational pull on the roast beef and beer re-surfacing in my throat. When the arm stopped in the dead vertical position to allow the opposing capsule to disembark at ground level

Patti and I were left suspended upside down in our harness high above the lights of Scottsdale. The sudden cessation of movement was the trigger that launched the contents of my gastric system earthward and that's about as much as I can remember until we were back on the bus.

The bus ride back to the ranch after a prom was traditionally a time for canoodling to cement new relationships, or not, depending on how the evening had gone. Most definitely the latter result in my case as I had proven myself to be about as distant from cool as it was possible to get, a position I had always been aware of myself but which Patti had only just discovered. She sat silently in the darkened bus that was now being lashed by the torrential rain of a desert storm. Had I felt sufficiently well I might have attempted to make amends but I was not up to it by a long shot and in any event I suspect I would have only dug the hole deeper.

Just before arriving at the ranch the un-metalled access road crosses the bed of Ash Creek. This watercourse was almost always dry at this point, the flow of water having gone underground, but as we approached it in the early hours of the post-prom morning the headlights of the bus lit up a raging flash flood of muddy water. Attempting to cross was out of the question so with great difficulty, given it was dark and dense mesquite bushes lined the track, the bus turned around and headed back out to the public highway some miles away. Reaching it we drove on, intending to try an approach along a dirt road entering the ranch from further north. Leaving the tarmac for this alternative route the bus immediately bogged down in gooey orange mud freshly made by the storm. We disembarked sleepily into the mire and with the sky lightening in the east began the long trudge through rock and prickly pear back to school. Our rag-tag group in its soiled and dishevelled finery must have looked like nothing so much as actors in a disaster movie playing the survivors of some horrible apocalypse. I don't think Pattie talked to me at any point on that long walk or even walked near me. In later years she went on to gain some notoriety as Patti Davis; actress, author, Playboy model and anti-nuclear activist. I occasionally wonder what might have been had I played my cards better.

Later in that summer of 1965 another problem of my own making arose at home in England. I would shortly be turning eighteen which meant that as a U.S. citizen (I had dual nationality) I would be required to sign with the draft board in Arizona for potential military duty. It was true that not many people in full-time education had been drafted at that stage but Johnson was ramping up the war in Vietnam month by month and nobody knew what might happen. I considered the situation. My genuine intention was to return to England permanently after graduating from high school. It therefore seemed an opportune time to renounce my U.S. citizenship.

Boarding school far from home had instilled an independent mind so, without consulting my parents or anyone else, I took the tube down to Grosvenor Square and told somebody at the US embassy what it was I wanted. After an interview regarding my reasoning I was told to come back for an appointment with a vice consul the following week. I returned on time and was ushered into a spacious office dominated by a huge polished desk. A dark-suited man was seated behind it reading some documents. He didn't look up. Above him on the wall was a large replica of the Great Seal of the United States with beside it a Stars and Stripes on a pole. I was announced by the usher who then instructed me to stand in front of the desk. The vice-consul, if that's who he was, stood up and finally favoured me with a brief glance. The usher placed a bible in my right hand and a printed sheet of words in my left. The vice-consul spoke solemnly without making eye contact and at the appropriate point his assistant indicated I should recite the printed declaration in my left hand. The vice consul sat down, my American passport was taken from me and I was rather curtly shown from the room.

A few days later I returned to the embassy with my British passport to apply for the visa I would now need to return for my final year at Orme. After a long wait my number was called and I pushed my passport and completed application form under the glass partition to the official behind it. He examined both and then appeared to consult a long list on a clipboard off to one side. He pushed passport and form back to me and fixed me with a stare.

"Problem?" I asked.

"Son" he said, "I believe you've recently renounced your US citizenship?"

"Yes, I did" I confirmed.

"Well, if I were you I wouldn't expect to ever again set foot in the United States of America."

Then he turned away to a microphone to call the number of the next applicant.

I was rather taken aback by what I saw as this rather vengeful attitude and returned to Fetter Lane to consult my father. *He* was rather taken aback that

        a) I hadn't discussed my intentions with him,

        b) the embassy had allowed me to do it and

        c) I could be so stupid.

There was about a month to go before I was due to fly back to Phoenix. My father worked as an editor for Reuters on Fleet Street. Over the years he had spent a lot of time on their North American desk, had interviewed many US politicians and inevitably had come to know a number of embassy officials. He went to work on the telephone.

We were both summoned to Grosvenor Square the following week. We waited together outside the same office I had attended previously. I was called first. It was the same man but this time he looked at me intensely. He did not seem pleased to see me again. With a noticeable economy of words he told me that my renunciation of citizenship would remain effective but would be post-dated to the day after my graduation, so allowing me to return to school for my final year. This, he said, was exceptional, adding that I would be obliged to leave the US immediately upon completion of the graduation ceremony. I was then dismissed and my father called in. He came out after a few minutes looking unusually shaken. Apparently he had been given a thorough dressing down and told there was a good case for stripping him of *his* nationality for being such a poor father as to allow his only son to resign membership of the greatest country in the world.

Back at Orme for a fourth and final year a sea change was occurring. We seniors were approaching adulthood (adultery if one of our number was to be believed, though that was almost certainly wishful thinking on his part). Our focus was tightening on the adult pleasures of women and stimulants. The latter were beer and bourbon rather than drugs because, despite our strong California connection, marijuana, cocaine and LSD had yet to penetrate to an isolated ranch in northern Arizona. Maybe our wholesome outdoor life in a close community was a factor in their absence, though I doubt it. It was just that it would take another year or two before drugs became ubiquitous throughout the whole schools system.

Our remote self-sufficiency had a lot to answer for in other respects though. Charlie Orme had always loved lecturing on the importance of our Judaeo-Christian heritage. Yet while he was talking of events 2000 years earlier Martin Luther King marched on Washington with his dream, Ken Kesey toured America popping acid with the Merry Pranksters, the Beatles went psychedelic, the anti-war movement was tearing the country apart, and the 'summer of love' approached. Apart from the music none of this world-changing social and political turmoil beyond Ash Creek seemed to get to us. It was all a long way away and we were too self-absorbed.

Most of my attention was absorbed by Joanie Roberts. As

with Patti it could only have been my effortless qualification as a Brit that persuaded her I might make interesting boyfriend material. Joanie was a long-legged California blonde and also represented quite a catch. Everyone was astonished, none more than me, at this development. The difficulty in all boy-girl situations at Orme was that the school had something called the HOP. This stood for 'hands off policy'. It meant that while you could associate freely with the opposite sex, talk to them, walk with them, eat with them and so on, you were not allowed to actually touch them in any sort of sexual way, not even to hold hands. Clearly this was unsatisfactory. Fortunately Ash Creek provided many secluded locations for *rendezvous* arranged in the hope of losing innocence and finding knowledge not officially listed on the curriculum.

My own strategy, after a few weeks of opening play, was to invite Joanie to a late-night *tete-a-tete* barbecue on Buzzard Peak, a rocky, cone-shaped hill just to the south of the ranch. During the afternoon I shot some wild quail (this was Arizona so of course we were allowed guns, although not in our rooms. They were kept in a central armoury but could be checked out at will- school massacres were a future horror). To facilitate what I hoped might be a transition from *tete-a-tete* to something even more intimate I negotiated the purchase of some alcohol from a fellow senior called Wilcox: a half bottle of Bombay gin, suitably British I thought. After the price was agreed and paid he described the bottle's hiding place in a hollow cottonwood near the creek. All was set. I slipped out of bounds in the dark with the plucked and gutted quail, wire coat hangers on which to roast them over a campfire, matches and the gin. I hoped Joanie would not stand me up. She didn't. I think the subsequent difficulties arose because, not being familiar with gin, I had neglected to take any dilutants. Consequently we swigged the stuff neat. Joanie was a good deal more experienced than I in matters of both booze and sex and proceeded with caution. I was not, and did not, with the inevitable result that a romantic barbecue deteriorated into an affair of burnt quail, awkward fumblings and a growing urge to throw up, in other words a situation not unlike the Patti debacle I had hoped to put behind me.

The return to school grounds proved as difficult as it had been on that earlier occasion. The boys' camp lay in the opposite direction to the girls' dormitories so I went off one way, Joanie another. Unfortunately my route lay across the site of the new school gymnasium where construction had advanced as far as the digging of deep trench foundations. Here and there these were bridged with boards provided for the passage of people and wheelbarrows. Even had I been aware of the existence of these there was no way I would have found them. I disappeared into the foundations. They were two metres deep so the top of my head was a good foot below ground level. The toxic effects of the gin prevented me from appreciating the proper nature of this severe disadvantage and I must have made two or three circuits of the extensive groundworks before realising I was making no forward progress at all. Determined not to spend the night like a mole I managed to clamber back up to the surface and, a bit muddy, continued unsteadily back to my quarters where I collapsed, fully clothed, under a running shower.

Just like Patti, Joanie had suffered a total disillusionment, so that was the end of that. She quickly found a more reliable replacement. A tall Californian who played American football. This prompted my friends, whenever they saw me with a gun, to launch into the mean-cool lyrics of the new Hendrix release *Hey Joe:*

> *Hey Joe, where you goin' with that gun of yours?*
> *Hey Joe, I said where you goin' with that gun in your hand,*
> *Oh I'm goin' down to shoot my old lady*
> *You know I caught her messin' 'round with another man*

It amused them and somehow the macho imagery cheered me up a bit.

As my return home to England approached it occurred that it might be sensible to equip myself with a driving licence obtained in Arizona. This required attendance with a vehicle at the Yavapai county sheriff's office in Mayer. Susie Hearst our English teacher had a red Triumph Spitfire: yet another manifestation of British cool but unlike me, one that could be relied on to operate smoothly. I asked her if I could use it for the test. She said that would be fine if I could make a convenient appointment. So a few days later, in hot sunshine under a blue Arizona sky, I drove us towards Mayer to meet a deputy. Humming along the smooth blacktop with the roof down I felt that things couldn't get much better. Shades of *Hotel California* (though that was yet to be released).

Mayer was a quiet little place of only a few hundred residents. No one was about. We pulled up outside a small cinder-block building baking in the sun behind a drooped Stars and Stripes. In the air-conditioned interior sat the deputy in a Stetson hat. I was expected. He handed me a questionnaire on driving law. I completed it in a minute or two and handed it back over his desk. He ran down it with a pencil ticking and occasionally crossing before throwing it to one side, apparently satisfied, or so I hoped. Getting to his feet he said "Let's go" and came around the desk to pull open the glass door for me. We went back out into the heat and stepped into the Spitfire. Susie stayed back in the office.

"Nice car" commented the deputy.

"English" I said.

"Those guys sure make 'em small."

He was having a second go at shutting the passenger door against the bulky gun holster on his hip. The roof was still down.

"When you're ready take her out onto the highway."

I did and drove a mile or so along it shifting up through the gears without incident. There was no other traffic.

"Okay head back now" said the deputy.

I shifted down to second, executed a U-turn (no need for a three-pointer) and drove back to the sheriff's office.

"Okay," said my examiner "but you forgot to position in

the centre lane when you turned off the highway. I'll pass
you but remember next time."
Back in England I drove for a year on my Arizona licence until I
finally passed my British test at the fourth attempt.

Then it was June and graduation and bye-bye America,
as specifically ordered in my case by the US government. There
was a final bash down in Phoenix on our last night together
before dispersing. Unbelievably I had found another girl to escort to this 'do', one who was not dissuaded by my previous
romantic history or, just possibly, was unaware of it. We had all
booked into a motel and stayed up all night drinking, 'necking'
as the term was at the time, talking and changing rooms. Some
people were ready to move beyond just necking. Mid-clinch on
top of a double bed my date whispered
"I take those little white pills, you know, every day."
I hadn't a clue what she was talking about, even less of how to
take advantage of it. The '60s had penetrated our world in ways
I had yet to understand: so much for my personal representation
of Cool Britannia. In the morning we drove out to Sky Harbour
airport and I boarded a TWA 707 to return to England, live with
my mother and work on a Suffolk farm.

RAT BAIT

Crouching at the eastern-most limit of the land the town stares with stoicism at a brown sea that has already taken half of it and will take the other half one night when wind and wave and moon conspire in apocalyptic flood. Fishing, drinking and shooting are the occupations of its menfolk. When easterlies keep the longshore boats winched high on the shingle beach the Mill and the Vic' and the Black Horse fill with blue-smocked fishermen short on words but long on patience, men suspicious of strangers. The sea is full of fish and the marshes are alive with the calls of wildfowl. Winter dawns and dusks are punctuated by the sound of gunfire. A visit to any one of the pubs will furnish you, should you want them, with a cod or a pair of ducks or, if you speak quietly, a brace of pheasants.

This is a cold coast, a flat coast, exposed to a traitorous sea of shifting banks and penetrating winds, chilling even in summer. Martello towers, concrete gun emplacements and rusted barbed wire stand witness to old threats from the east. The new one faces banks of anti-aircraft missiles lining the low sandy cliffs behind MOD signs prohibiting entry. Just above the waves American jets thunder in to their bases close behind the shoreline. A few of the Yanks frequent the fishermen's pubs and are accepted for their friendly ways and profligate spending.

In these pubs in the '50s and '60s my father was in his element. He had a reporter's curiosity for people's stories. He empathises with his countrymen, argues baseball, politics and American football. But he loved the English. He married one. We lived in the town and it was through my father I got to know

Sugs.

Sugs occcasionally came up to our house for my father's Sunday morning get togethers. A heavy-set man with a square fleshy face, small ears and piggy eyes he wore a permanent grin enhanced by his only two teeth that pushed his bottom lip out and down. He wore a cloth cap that when removed in our kitchen revealed a hairless white plateau contrasting sharply with the reds and blues of his nose and jowls. What he had been in life I never found out because he was always reticent about his past. Not that he was very coherent about the present because drink had reduced his circumstances and his faculties to the degree that he was pretty washed up. I think Dad had been trying to help him a bit. Washed up too in the sense that he lived in a derelict Yarmouth shrimper the '53 floods had left stranded on the marshes a long way from the river. It's still there now but abandoned; the *Maid Marian*, a small, tarred, clinker-built thing with mast and rigging long gone and its deck caved in. Sugs didn't own it but paid a rent of five shillings a week to one of the fishermen. He owed quite a lot of back rent. I think that was what Dad helped him with.

Sugs's big problem with the boat, apart from the rent, and the damp, was the rats. The marshes are full of them. When the dykes and ditches froze up in winter Sugs's home represented a little oasis of warmth and food that no rat worth the name could ignore. Its largely rotten hull was no barrier to rodent teeth and so Sugs found himself sharing his sparse food supplies and scant living space with his fellow marsh-dwellers. Initially he bought a rat-sized version of the 'Little Nipper' mousetrap. If you've used 'Little Nippers' you'll know the proper setting of them requires a steady hand and iron nerves, attributes alcohol denied Sugs.

Displaying his bruised fingers in the Black Horse he wondered if they might be broken but was soon assured it would take more than a 'Little Nipper' to break those sausage-like digits.

"What you want bor is a proper gin trap" said Toots, one

of the fishermen, "that'll sort the buggers. I'll bring you one out of my shed tomorrow."

"Toots you'll get our ole mate here arrested" said Sperry who worked for Coypu Control and knew about traps "gin traps is illegal nowadays."

"Not for rats they in't," answered Toots and a long discussion followed on the efficacy of various kinds of traps and other weird and wonderful ways of murdering rodents. The one consistency was agreement on the idiocy of those in authority.

Toots brought his gins into the Horse the following day and, after casting an eye around to make sure no strangers were present, demonstrated their setting and springing to Sugs. The serrated jaws clacked shut with a frightening ferocity. Toots's theory was that when a rat felt the trigger plate start to give it would jump to escape, only to be caught in mid-air. He finished with a warning.

"Don't you get yer pinkies in there either Sugsie or they *will* get brook!"

Back at the Maid Marian the setting of the traps reduced Sugs to a nervous wreck. When he finally got them set and positioned they were set so coarsely a herd of coypu might have marched across them without incident. Toots eventually came down to help but was humbled when his theory was proved fanciful: the rats sprung the traps but the jaws always missed them.

"These here marsh rats is clever little sods" was his conclusion.

Frustrated, Sugs decided to revert to the reliability of the marshman's time-honoured weapon, the shotgun. Sensibly he borrowed a single shot .410 after deciding he would be overgunned with the old hammer 12 bore he occasionally used on any ducks foolish enough to alight on the marsh within range of the boat's one functioning porthole. Unfortunately he delayed his armed vigil until after the Horse had shut. Consequently as he sat by candlelight beside his bunk, shotgun across his lap, neither his vision nor his aim was at peak performance. Suddenly and silently a rat appeared on the cabin floor. The candlelight glittered in its little button-black eyes. Sugs fired. Temporarily deafened, he peered through the smoke and dust for the rodent's body. There was no sign of one but roughly where the rat had been was a large hole in the boat's hull, the oozy mud below reflecting the candlelight. The rats were winning by a mile.

Sugs's attempt to get even was bizarre. He never talked about his wartime life, with good reason. He had served with Wingate's 'Forgotten Army' in Burma and had been taken prisoner by the Japanese. That experience was generally reckoned by his mates to have led to his need for the comforting amnesia induced by beer. It had also somehow left him in possession of a Japanese officer's ceremonial sword. This was an ornate weapon, very heavy, exceptionally sharp and with a fine point. Sugs suspended it from the cabin ceiling with two lengths of binder twine secured to cuphooks. A third length of string was tied to the sword's handle, led around another cuphook in the cabin wall and back across the cabin to a nail hammered up through a shelf on the opposite wall. Putting tension on this string pulled the sword back and up to the 'loaded' position. The nail end of the string was then tied securely around a piece of hard cheese impaled on the nail. The idea was that when a rat began gnawing it the cheese would be dislodged from the nail, the sword would descend at speed and the rat would be skewered. Sugs demonstrated this Poe-like mechanism to me and it did look good, the sword flying across the cabin and burying its tip in the wall with a satisfying thump as the hilt vibrated impressively. Yet the danger of the trapper becoming the trapped was obvious, especially after a trip to the Horse. I once made this point to Sugs who said that as the sword hadn't got him for the three years he had observed it in the hands of the camp commander it wasn't likely to get him now. Nor did it. After he had failed to show up at the Horse for two days Toots found him slumped at the cabin table, dead from a heart attack. It looked as if he had just eaten a meal of fish and chips. At least we hoped he had.

A FARMER'S BOY

Freddie Stigwood was a cut above the average farmer. As principal tenant on the Blackheath estate he lived in Friston Hall and farmed a thousand acres of the surrounding land. Most of this was the light sandy soil of the Suffolk coast with occasional intrusions of clay, a combination allowing Freddie to grow the full range of traditional arable crops from beans to rye to potatoes. This he did with a keen eye to the agricultural technology that was racing ahead in the 1960s. Nor was he shy of investing in it. He had the most powerful tractors, the biggest combine harvester and the highest profile of any farmer in the district. Which is why one August day in 1966, not without trepidation, I rode my Honda 50 moped up the long drive to Friston Hall to ask for a job.

Numbering around fourteen Freddie's workforce was considered small for the large acreage he farmed. It contained a number of superior technicians, men who knew all about spraying and complicated mechanics. Traditional old hand-workers who couldn't drive a tractor but knew how to build a corn stack or lay a hedge were poorly represented. There didn't seem much hope Freddie would employ a nineteen-year-old boy like me, one with an almost total ignorance of farming. But my mother, a spirited woman, had impressed on me the reasoning that 'you won't know if you don't ask'. In the event Freddie Stigwood had not only a need for some extra harvest help but also a generous character that allowed him to give me the benefit of the doubt and a job. It wasn't long before he wished he hadn't.

I started off well enough over the first couple of weeks,

driving trailers loaded with barley or wheat from the harvest fields back to the farmyard at Friston. Here I would reverse them up to the intake pit and tip the load of grain under the supervision of a man called Hordy who looked after its drying and storage. Having been driving for several years in Arizona I was not unduly daunted by tractors and seemed reasonably competent at accurate reversing. I had also quickly acquired the knack of driving at the right speed and distance beside the combine harvester as it unloaded into my trailer without stopping. All in all I felt I was coping rather well with my first proper job.

The first disaster was a fire. Here and there across the extensive barley stubbles behind Friston Hall the level expanse was broken by occasional clumps of straw. These were bales come adrift and left behind when the fields were cleared. Before ploughing could commence they had to be burnt to get them out of the way, a sufficiently simple job for an inexperienced boy. Or at least one with enough sense to anticipate the effect of wind and flame on over a hundred contiguous acres of dry stubble. Thinking I would deal with the farthest field first I set fire to a broken bale a half a mile or so from the farmyard. The result was spectacular. As the flames raced toward the first hedge a huge pall of black smoke churned skyward. It looked doubtful that I could get back to the farmyard before the flames reached it but I thought I should at least try, if only to warn someone at the Hall of their imminent incineration. The first person I could find was Hordy. He came out of the grain store to have a look.

"Goo ta Hell bor" he said, calmly staring at the black smoke that was now over the yard "tha's gonna make a rum mess o' the ole gal's washin'."
This was blowing about in the strong wind in the garden of the Hall behind us. Smuts of burnt straw were beginning to fill the air.

"Nevermind the washing" I said, "what are we going to do? Shall we telephone the fire brigade?"
I was slightly less panicked now the situation was under the

supervision of someone senior.

"Don't you worry bor" said Hordy "that'll burn isself out in a few minutes. Wot you want a be a worryin' about is that that look to me like you might ha' burned that bit o' ole hedge jus' where Cap'n Wentworth allus stand when he's shootin' partridges. Tha's his favourite drive, he in't gonna be very happy if he find that in't there."
I didn't know whether he was pulling my leg or not.

The fire did not damage my standing too much. Although dramatic nobody was hurt and nothing of value was destroyed, although I presume the washing had to be re-washed. Sitting around in the shed where we took our meal breaks one or two of the men said in my defence it might have been foolish of the boss to put a boy on such a job on a dry day when the wind was likely to get up. The silence of the others indicated they thought any boy with half a brain would have known better.

That opinion certainly won the day the following week when my tractor-driving skills deserted me. After a day of spring-tining ploughed land ready to drill with rye I brought my tractor back to the yard and parked it in the big implement shed. Or more exactly half in it because I failed to appreciate how high the front loading arm of the tractor was lifted. I manoeuvred it through the double doors of the shed without incident but then, in paying too much attention to the amount of space I had behind me, I rammed the loader out through a wall. This necessitated expensive repairs to wall and machine. To his credit Freddie did not let these two incidents prevent him from giving me further chances to prove myself. These were wasted.

At that time, 1966, Friston Hall had one of the biggest, most powerful tractors available, a Fordson County Super Six with a modern luxury cab. In appearance it was a strikingly impressive blue monster, notable for having front wheels the same size as its massive rear ones. Freddie allocated me this shiny new machine one morning and set me off harrowing a large field near Friston. There was a house in the middle of the field, its long straight drive splitting the enclosure in half. Freddie said I should ignore the presence of this drive or else I would create extra 'headlands' with all the turning back and forth. Rather I should lift the harrows each time I reached the drive, cross it and drop the harrows back into work on the other side. They were very large modern harrows with hydraulically operated folding 'wings' out to either side. I soon got the hang of it, lifting the control lever just enough for the harrows to clear the surface of the drive as I crossed and thrusting it back down again once they were over.

I must have got quite cocky perched high on this new tractor with the radio in the cab blasting out loud music from Radio Caroline. I kept increasing the revs to go faster and faster as I progressed across the field. What I had not realised was that the higher the revs the more rapidly the hydraulic rams on the harrow operated: the 'wings' were lifting to a position increasingly near the vertical each time I crossed the drive. Eventually just after crossing it for the umpteenth time the big tractor began to behave oddly, belching black smoke from the exhaust as if it was overloaded. I gave it a bit more throttle. All four enormous wheels began to spin. It was only then that I looked behind me to see that the wings of the harrow had lifted to a height sufficient to snag the telephone cable that was slung on poles running up the drive. The shiny copper cable, stripped of its insulation, was stretched as tight as a banjo string from the tractor to the several poles to which it was still attached. These were leaning towards me at an angle of about 30 degrees to the ground.

I lifted the harrows very gently and reversed far enough to release the tension. After I had disentangled the cable it lay in long loose coils on the ploughed field like some monstrous murdered snake. My first thought was to walk up the drive to the house to inform the occupants that their telephone might not be working properly. My second thought was that it was lucky it hadn't been electricity.

Freddie Stigwood was very considerate of my feelings after these various mishaps. He explained that he had agreed to take on another farm at Michaelmas, Knodishall Hall, and that part of the deal was to continue the employment of the men working there. Because of that, he said, he would have to let me go on a 'last in first out' basis. I'm sure he was more than a little relieved to be rid of me.

At the beginning of November I found another job, eight or ten miles away at Wenhaston. This was not so much a move forwards, or even sideways, but backwards several decades. From the cutting edge of agricultural technology on the wide acres of Friston Hall I had moved to a small mixed farm working closer to the traditions of Elizabethan times. Old Hall was owned and farmed by Stuart Onyett who lived in the medieval farmhouse with his mother and a live-in New Zealand cowman called Brian. On my first day Stuart was quick to tell me that after he had agreed to employ me he had phoned Freddie Stigwood for a reference and had been informed of my inexperience. Consequently he doubted whether he would be able to pay me the full weekly amount for a nineteen-year-old as stipulated by the Agricultural Wages Board. I pointed out that we had already agreed terms and, in any event, £7.10s. was little enough for a five and a half day week. Stuart said he would have to see. This rather set the tone for my employment.

In any case no great deal of experience was required for my primary duties of shovelling cow muck into a wheelbarrow and feeding the pigs. Yet as with all jobs there were some knacks to be learned. One of these was to master the Suffolk dialect as spoken by Billy, the farm's only other employee apart from Brian and myself. Billy was a proper old timer who helped out with any handwork but spent most of the winter cutting and laying hedges, a steady few yards each day. He always wore the same knee-length brown coat under a round tweed hat waterproofed with grease. On my second or third day I was eating my mid-morning bun perched on a straw bale several feet up in the pole barn when I saw Billy approaching across the yard.

"Ha' yer done the nettus?" asked Billy looking up at me.

"Sorry?" I said looking back blankly.

"Ha' yer done the nettus?" he repeated.

I couldn't get it. Nettus? What was that? Lettuce? We didn't grow any lettuce as far as I knew.

"Sorry Billy, what . . .?"

"The nettus," shouted Billy "the cows!"

I finally got it. 'Neat', the old word for cows as in neatsfoot oil. Nettus, neat-house. Had I mucked out the milking parlour.

"Yes, yes, I have" I answered Billy who walked off across the yard shaking his head in disbelief that Stuart could have employed an idiot.

One of the farm's enterprises was to fatten pigs. Stuart would buy in weaners at eight to ten weeks old and house them in various looseboxes scattered around the yards. Here they would be fed barley grown on the farm until they were heavy enough to go to market in Ipswich. Each loosebox had an iron feeding trough or two and it was my job to carry a bucket of barley meal and a bucket of water to tip into each of these troughs twice each day. This was not as easy as it might sound because the pigs could hear me coming. They would begin an hysterical squealing, piling up against the lower half of the loosebox doors in a frenzy of anticipation. Their weight against the door would make it very difficult to shoot the bolt to get in with the meal and water. The procedure I developed was to balance on one foot, a heavy bucket in each hand, while lifting my other foot to give the bolt a sharp kick. The result was usually an avalanche of pigs tumbling out of the door but with any luck they would follow me back in to get at their food.

The problem then was that the iron troughs would usually be upside down and jammed full of mucky straw. If I could not right them and clear them with footwork I was in trouble: putting down the buckets meant the pigs would upend them, water and meal vanishing into the straw. Even in the favourable circumstances of finding the trough empty of muck and the right way up, the contents of the buckets would cascade over the heads of the jostling pigs, never reaching the intended target. One or two animals, perhaps those with a particularly acute sense of smell or a higher intelligence, could, on falling out of a loosebox door, sense the location of the main meal cache which was at the far end of a narrow building forming one side of the yard. These *alpha* pigs would set off at a run, negotiating two doorways and a long passage *en route* to end up snout deep in the big heap of meal. It would then be almost impossible to get them back to their pen until they became virtually catatonic from binge feeding. On reflection you had to admire their initiative but at the time a lot of swearing and chasing about condemned them as stupid bloody creatures and worse. Occasionally a whole pen-full would follow these enterprising leaders leaving me standing in an empty loosebox with my two full buckets. At least in that situation I could calmly fill the troughs in the intended manner.

The pigs lost a good deal of my sympathy, and Stuart a good bit more, when a group of weaners ate my wages. Mucking out one of the looseboxes on a Saturday morning I had worked up a sweat sufficient to remove my old army surplus jacket and hang it over the bottom half of an adjacent pen door. That was very foolish because the pen was full of young pigs that, unobserved by me, removed the coat that contained in a pocket the £7.10s. Stuart had just paid me. The coat was exactly what the pigs needed to relieve their boredom with a tug of war, and their hunger with scraps of cloth and pound notes. Not a trace, not a button, was left.

I reported the disaster to Stuart who was lunching indoors with Brian and his mother. He thought it tremendously funny but equally hard luck. I suggested he might re-pay my wages and claim on the farm's insurance. This he found nearly as funny as my misfortune. Painfully conscious I had worked a whole five and a half days for absolutely nothing, worse, I had lost my coat, I attempted to rescue some advantage by asking if I could have the trailer load of manure I had spent the morning digging out of the loosebox. Stuart screwed up his face in worried thought. He had a squashed sort of face with very little distance between his lower lip and his chin.

"How would you get it home?" he asked me.

"Couldn't I borrow the tractor?" I said "and take a bag of 20.10.10 as well?" This last was fertilizer, which, with the manure, would greatly benefit my mother's vegetable garden.

"Well all right," said Stuart "but make sure you get it back before dark."

The following Saturday morning I opened a wage packet for the first time in two weeks to find a single 10s. note and a scribbled piece of paper reading:

Wages	£7.10s.0d.
Hire of tractor and diesel	£2.0s.0d.
Load of muck	£3.0s.0d.
Bag of fertilizer	£2.0s.0d.
Total	£7.0s.0d.

This did nothing to enhance Stuart's standing with me but nonetheless I was pleased when one bright January morning he announced he would teach me to plough with the old Fordson tractor. Normally Stuart did the ploughing so this seemed a privilege, making a change from my routine of feeding the animals at their front ends and clearing away the results at the other. The farm had only an old-fashioned one-way plough instead of the new reversible type everyone else was using, so there was some skill involved in 'setting up the tops' and 'finishing the bottoms' properly. Stuart stayed with me long enough to get me started and then disappeared, leaving me slowly grinding up and down a field of kale that had been grazed off by the cows. The Fordson had no protective cab, so when in late morning the sun was obscured by low cloud the colour of sheet metal, the cold became intense. By the time it started to snow I realised Stuart's enthusiasm to teach me the skills of ploughing had not been entirely selfless.

I carried on at Old Hall into the summer determined to complete a year's experience of practical agriculture. This was a

prerequisite for entry to the Royal Agricultural College at Cirencester, the establishment I decided would best serve my needs
in becoming a land agent, an occupation I thought might suit
me in the absence of a family farm. By now, despite my nominal
wages, I had managed by reason of living at home to save enough
to buy a proper motorbike, a Honda 305cc Superhawk. This
made the early morning commute to Wenhaston much more
exciting until one morning, accelerating away from a sharp
bend, the wing of a VW Beetle appeared from a driveway in front
of me. Regaining consciousness, my eyes focused on a large pair
of shiny black boots on the tarmac just in front of them. A voice
from one of the southern American states drawled

"Are yah awlright kid?"
An American serviceman from the airbase. The Honda lay in
the middle of the road fairly well dis-assembled. Some people
came out from the house opposite and an ambulance was called
despite my only serious injury being a broken wrist. A little
later my mother called Stuart to tell him I would not be in.

"Damn" he said, "I'll have to go and feed the pigs."

A letter arrived from Cirencester inviting me to an interview with the principal, Frank Garner, at the Farmers' Club in
London. This posh private members' club is situated just off
Whitehall close to the seats of power. I was shown into a small
oak-panelled room and introduced to Garner. After quizzing
me about my background and intentions for the future he got
around to asking what G.C.E 'A' Levels I had achieved: at least
two were stipulated as a requirement for entry to the college,
although I suspect this condition might have been modified if
a candidate was in possession of an appropriate family name
or title. I was not well armed for this, having neither social
leverage nor 'A Level' certificates. A high school diploma was all
I could offer and I could see from Garner's slightly averted look
that this didn't cut the mustard, despite my assurances that I

had scored highly enough in the US to be accepted at some of their leading universities. Well, that's that I thought. Then Garner asked me where I had completed my year's practical experience. I stressed the progressive situation at Friston Hall and then reluctantly mentioned Old Hall.

"Old Hall Wenhaston" declared Garner, surprised, "Stuart Onyett?!"

"Yes" I said, not sure what was coming next.

"Good Lord" said Garner "as a boy I spent all my summer holidays there in a caravan with my parents. Good Lord!"
And that was that. I was in.

DAVID

David always wore a faded corduroy sports jacket and an air of barely repressed arrogance. His superior demeanour was assisted by a tall thin frame and a vaguely feminine bone structure hinting at centuries of marrying second cousins. His triple surname, de Clarenson Leatham, gave an authentic ring to the affectation. David claimed it went back to the Conquest. His father was the very model of a modern major general and lived in Sussex near Arundel. Yet anyone hoodwinked into thinking any of this was the manifestation of a gentleman would be badly fooled, for David was an unprincipled rogue. If he really had any blue blood it came from a robber baron, not a benevolent country squire.

Quite how or why we became friends escapes me now. A shared interest in fishing and shooting might have helped, but then almost everyone at the Royal Agricultural College had that in common. More likely, despite his charade of establishment elitism, David was drawn to those who broke the mold of our fellow students, most of whom were heirs of the landed classes. I was certainly not one of those, as David was wont to remind me often enough.

"You wouldn't understand" he would say "being a colonial, or a half-colonial at any rate. An American father! Tut, tut!" I would take this as a jest but I was never altogether sure he didn't believe in his own nonsense. In later life his assumed superiority mutated to Christian evangelism. He became a minister of the Baptist church, though only briefly before his renegade views had him defrocked.

At college a useful application of David's manner and appearance was in the seeking of student accommodation. By the end of our first autumn term my landlady had died (of causes unrelated to my presence) and David had decided the college halls were not for him. Our technique was to drive the back roads of the Cotswolds seeking the expansive honey-coloured manor houses for which the region is well known. On spotting a nice one we would park David's Triumph Herald convertible on the gravel opposite the timeworn oak of the front door before giving the iron bell-pull a confident tug. Usually this would set a terrier or two yapping somewhere in a distant hallway, often accompanied by a cry along the lines of 'Oh Annabelle, Trixie, do shut up!' before the door would be opened. Sometimes by a maid, sometimes by the lady of the house in hunting kit and occasionally by a silver-haired patriarch of military bearing. In whichever case this was the signal for David to launch into a cunning and cringe-inducing introduction.

This speech was a masterpiece of combined hubris and humility, referring both to our presence at a renowned institution for the privileged classes, while bemoaning the difficulty faced by underfunded students in finding 'suitable' accommodation. Did the estate perhaps have a cottage or flat that might be available to the right sort of tenants? Inevitably the pivotal role played by David's father in British military affairs would surface within the first few minutes of interview, the information imparted with an upper class stutter modulated to suit David's assessment of our host's social standing. These sorties usually came to nothing, although we did enjoy numerous cups of tea drunk from fine china and, on one occasion, champagne. But we only needed one success and eventually we had it.

Mrs de Saumerez had married well, divorced and come away from the settlement with a large property set in several acres of parkland. Her maiden name was Wilson, her family came from Croydon and she fell for David's ploy hook, line and sinker. Daglingworth Manor had a spacious three-bedroom self-contained flat over one wing of the house and this she agreed to let to us for £5 a week. Behind the house we had noticed the surface of a small lake was stippled with rising trout as pheasants and a peacock strutted the surrounding lawns. In painting a picture of ourselves as young country gentlemen of breeding we had mentioned fly-fishing as one of our preferred dalliances with the desired result:

"Well do feel free to try your luck occasionally" said Mrs de S., "though I fear you'll find it too easy- no one ever fishes for them."

Cock-a-hoop we agreed some details, rounded up a couple of mates to share the flat and moved in. Within a week or two we had emptied the lake of trout and purged the grounds of pheasants, leaving the peacock for later. Nevertheless Mrs de S. failed to twig the true nature of her tenants and all continued well. For a time.

A large dovecote stood centrally in the front courtyard of the house and in this lived a small flock of white fantails. On Saturdays David usually called on Mrs de S. to pay our rent. On one such occasion she voiced her fear that her birds had been corrupted by immigrants: bits of black or blue had begun to appear in the white plumage of the current year's offspring. This was a terrible shame, she said, as the purity of their fluttery whiteness added so much to the ambience of the house (she pronounced 'ambience' as if she were French). Sensing a so far overlooked opportunity David offered to investigate the problem.

Towards midnight that night, armed with a torch and an airgun, we climbed out through a skylight onto the roof of the house where we found the multi-coloured feral pigeons roosting on the ridge. They were sitting ducks. Over a period of two or three nights David and I despatched the lot for incorporation into pigeon casseroles. We reported back to Mrs de S. 'mission accomplished'. She was most grateful. We failed to mention that a number of the white doves, possibly impressed with the hybrid virility of the interlopers, had taken to roosting beside them on the roof. In the interests of thorough ethnic cleansing we had thought it best to take these out as well. The final result was that the few remaining white doves had fled for their lives and the dovecote stood forlornly empty. I think it was at about this time that Mrs de S. realised she had unwittingly housed a nest of vipers.

Things came to a head one Sunday evening when David was only slightly dilatory in paying the week's rent. There was a peremptory knock on the door to the flat before it was flung open by a clearly agitated Mrs de S., her cheeks flushed with anger.

"Where is Mr. Leatham" she shouted.

"I am here," replied David appearing in the doorway of his bedroom.

"What have you done with my doves?"

"Restored their racial purity as you wished."

"They've gone- what have you done with them?"

"I must say I haven't noticed them fluttering about recently. I wonder if there's a peregrine about."

"Peregrine! Peregrine! Rubbish! What have you done with them, you, you, you...?"

"I'm afraid I'm at a loss."

"No Mr Leatham, I am the one at a loss. And on that point where is my rent?"

We flatmates well knew that David saw verbal confrontations of this sort not so much as opportunities for rapprochement as duels to the death. Mrs de S. was an innocent to the slaughter.

"Ah yes. I'm afraid I was obliged to use this week's rent to buy a replacement element for the immersion heater. That, I believe, is your responsibility as landlord."

This was a complete fiction. For a moment Mrs de S. was dumbstruck. She quickly recovered.

"You've no right to do that!"

"I'm afraid I have," said David "and I have."

The three of us co-tenants stood beside and slightly behind

David unsure as to how this drama might unfold for Mrs de S. was now in danger of losing it altogether.

"You poncey scarecrow!" said Mrs de S., nee Wilson, "the lot of you are a bunch of stuck-up liars. I want you all out of my house!"

"I don't believe there is any need to become abusive," said David "but if you wish to serve three months notice as stipulated in our contract we will of course receive it."

"Too bloody right you will" said Mrs de S. "first thing in the morning!"

"In the meantime," said David, back-tracking in the face of this development, "as a gesture of goodwill we are prepared to pay this week's rent over and above the expenditure we have incurred on your behalf."

At this David opened his jacket, took his wallet from an inside pocket and withdrew a £5 note. With a theatrical gesture he proffered it to Mrs de S. who made to take it from his hand. As she did so David raised his forearm, withdrawing the note from her reach.

"On one condition," said David "that you apologise for calling us liars."

This was absurd but it left Mrs de S. in a quandary: she wanted the £5 but she did not want to apologise. Seeing her hesitation David decided to go for broke and holding one end of the note fluttered it in front of her. She made a grab for it but not quickly enough to get hold of it before David jerked it back.

"I didn't hear anything," said David slowly extending the note towards Mrs de S. once more. She grabbed, David withdrew and this rapid-fire exchange continued for two or three more see-saw movements before Mrs de S. managed to get hold of her end of the note just as David pulled back. The note tore in half.

"Now you foolish woman, you see what greed and stubbornness achieves" said David "you will have to sellotape it together."

Mrs de S. screwed her half of the banknote into a small ball and hurled it at David's face before turning on her heel and storming

out of the flat shouting

"You hooligans will be hearing from my solicitor!"
David unscrewed the ball of half £5 note and went in search of some sticky tape.

We served out our period of notice in a reduced version of the Cold War, Mrs de S. avoiding confrontation for fear of suffering further damage to her ego. She sensed, as we knew, that David was itching to explode more of his arsenal in retaliation for our eviction. Surprisingly the peacock still strutted the lawns unaware of its now even more precarious situation. In an effort at distraction we sent David off to find replacement accommodation. None of our subsequent landlords fared much better than had Mrs de Saumerez.

As he was not an Old Etonian David was excluded from that college clique which best reflected his attitude to studies. For in common with most of those heirs of the establishment David only attended lectures when he could think of no amusing alternative. This caused him some concern in our third year when he came to the realisation that any Etonians leaving without gaining professional qualification were nonetheless likely to enjoy a far greater financial security than he could anticipate. Consequently he began to borrow my lecture notes. As further insurance against failure he also mounted a charm offensive against our various tutors, the most susceptible being the forestry lecturer Dr. Hunt who revelled in his official title as 'The Queen's Verderer of the Forest of Dean'. He was a silly, pompous little man who knew a lot about trees and the intricacies of the royal family but not much about people. He was a sitting duck for David who would sidle up to him on a field trip to ask some inane question which, with its answer, was calculated to allow references to the doctor's relations with the Queen, the rank of David's father and David's abiding and passionate love of trees. This was all fair enough, I thought, if he could get away with it.

For myself I was confident that my comprehensive grasp of the forestry syllabus, my best and favourite subject, would deliver me that year's Silver Cup for Forestry. What I did not anticipate was that the self-important Hunt would be sufficiently flattered by David to award that pretender the cup. It still hurts.

After three years, feeling we had done our bit to uphold the traditions for which the college was famous, we dispersed in pursuit of careers. Those without estates to run took junior jobs with firms of land agents. David had decided he was not prepared for subservience, so instead requisitioned his father's remote fishing cottage in the hills of Galloway. Here he set up as a professional beekeeper and benefits fraudster. We were both in our mid twenties and reading voraciously in an effort to resolve how to be and what to do: it was the early '70s and a whiff of revolution had penetrated even our rural climes. Thoreau, Kerouac, Ken Kesey, Adrian Bell, Richard Brautigan, John Stewart Collis- we consumed an eclectic mix of trippy Americans and sober English ruralists. Living at opposite ends of the country I saw David only occasionally when I travelled north hoping for a bit of fishing.

On one early visit it was clear Thoreau and *Walden Pond* had got the upper hand: minimalism was the order of the day. For some reason I can't recall David had decided this ascetic philosophy would somehow be encouraged by painting the ceilings of the cottage black and the walls aubergine. The effect was unrelentingly depressing. In a further effort to suppress his material requirements David scrupulously adhered to a principle of living off the land, refusing to purchase, at least by means of money, any foodstuffs with the one exception of Jacob's cream crackers, to which he appeared addicted. For the visitor this combination of décor and diet was only tolerable for one or two nights unless the fishing was particularly good.

David was aided in his daily pursuit of food by a dog given

to him by the estate gamekeeper. This was a young, tail-less Labrador that had lost its rear appendage in a traffic incident, thus eliminating itself from the usual market for these pedigree animals. David named it Hoodlum, which became a self-fulfilling prophecy as he expected it to live by the same Thoreauvian principles he had adopted for himself. In other words he never actually bought any food for it, rebuffing any accusations of cruelty with 'it's a dog for heaven's sake- thousands of years of evolution have designed it to live by hunting'. The reality was that all the talk of philosophy and principle was a typical David deceit constructed to provide cover for unmitigated meanness. As it was, Hoodlum took to the imposed regime with enthusiasm, developing into a lean, high-speed killing machine. To avoid his own eviction from the region David managed to persuade it not to molest farm livestock but anything else was fair game. It even learnt to catch fish, hurling itself onto the small pike that basked on the surface of the Black Burn behind the cottage. Rabbits and pheasants were its staple, usually run down at lightning speed. A tug of war would follow between dog and master, Hoodlum growling possessive defiance through a mouthful of feathers or fur while David pulled on a wing or leg, determined to wrest a proprietorial share of the kill. If he was master it was only in name.

Further contradictory nomenclature occurred when one of our former flatmates appointed David his best man. The wedding was on the groom's farm near Hereford. Some of us were staying the weekend in one of the farm's cottages and were enjoying the sun in the garden when David pulled up after a long drive down from Scotland. I walked over to greet him as he opened the back of his hatchback. A black streak passed between us at waist height, landed at a run and was gone.

"I think you should have that dog," said David "it's just the sort of animal for you."
I laughed at the absurdity of the idea, knowing just the sort of animal it was. By now it had disappeared beyond the gently rolling horizon of red Herefordshire soil, intent on running down

something edible.

The wedding went off successfully despite a fear prevalent amongst some of us that David's speech might result in the bride making a run for it, or at least David being dragged from the marquee and beaten by the groom's family. In the event his comments, though involving butter and Anchorites, passed without uproar. We all thought it was a cop out given his previous form. The next morning I came downstairs in the cottage to find a tall girl called Tara Tree (of whom more later) frying bacon. It was still quite early. Sitting to one side of the stove, watching the frying pan attentively was Hoodlum.

"David not up yet?" I said.

"Oh yes," replied Tara Tree " he's been up and left, back to Scotland. He said you were to have the dog."

And that was that. I couldn't leave it there, nor was I going to drive all the way up to Scotland to return it. It lay sprawled across the back seat of my car as I drove home to York. The unexpected richness of pickings snaffled from the wedding feast had overwhelmed its digestive tract. At regular intervals it produced silent seepages of gas of such strength I was forced to travel with all windows open. David would be feeling very pleased with himself.

WALKING THE LINE

T hese days I sometimes find an excuse to avoid going to a party. The reverse was true in my youth when I was more prone to gate-crash them, although distance occasionally seemed an obstacle.

For instance one Saturday evening in my early twenties I was sitting at my father's kitchen table, feeling resigned to the imminent arrival of *his* dinner guests. One was to be my ex-headmaster (the Irish alcoholic export previously referred to), a man implicated in several childhood traumas. Washing up at the sink was our ageing retainer Peggy Nightingale, present to assist my stepmother with the evening's hospitality. Her name may sound like something from *The Diary of an Edwardian Lady* but it's the truth. Peggy looked over her shoulder.

"Oi've sin happier faces at a wake"

"I'd rather it was"

"Tha's a poor way fer a young'un to be a-talkin'" said Peggy turning back to the dishes.
I said that I knew of a party in Sheffield but that was over two hundred miles away.

"Whoi are yer sittin' there then?" said Peggy into the sink.

"I wouldn't get there before midnight Peggy!"

"That'll jis be gooin' nicely b'then. Goo on, git orf out of it!"
Shamed by the old lady's energetic optimism I snaffled a bottle of dry Martini from my father's bar and set off in my Morris Mini

pickup.

At about 10.30pm on the A1 somewhere north of New-ark I thought it time to get the party started with a small swig of the Martini. Believe me, this had nothing to do with my being suddenly ambushed by an unexpected roundabout with a car crossing to my left. Rather than braking hard I slipped across in front of it. The other car braked hard instead. And then followed me round. Foolishly I'd failed to notice that the vehicle I'd just cut up was what, in the vernacular of the time, we called 'a jam sandwich'. This was a long time ago before the police had aggressive 4x4s. I think it might even have been an Allegro. Nonetheless it managed to overtake me and turned on the POLICE STOP sign mounted in its rear window. The officer walked back and then had to bend double to look through the small open rectangle of the Mini's sliding window. The horizon-tal Martini bottle lying parallel to the handbrake glared back at him.

"Having a party are we sir?" asked the officer.

"Not yet, on my way to one" I replied cheerily.

"Bit late isn't it?"

"I'm hoping it's an all-nighter."

"Where is it?"

"Rotherham somewhere."

"That's a long way from here."

"I know."

"You best get going then."

And that was that. Sometimes life surprises you and it's best not to query it.

GUNNERSIDE

I arrived at the top of Swaledale late on a Sunday evening after a long drive from the Suffolk coast. Three sports cars were already parked in front of the cottage on the hillside below the lodge. Two MGBs and an Alfa Romeo. As soon as I turned off the engine of my Mini I could hear the laughter and strident voices of their owners coming through the open front door. I walked in to find six young men of about my own age sprawled across sofas and chairs in a cramped living room. They held cans of beer in their hands. My sudden appearance in the doorway provoked a momentary silence.

"Hello," I tried "is this the loaders' cottage?"
A lanky-looking fellow with one leg hooked over the side of his armchair answered. He was resting a can of McEwan's Export on his stomach.

"Yes, but it's full."

"Oh" I said "I'm loading too so where am I supposed to go?"

"No idea, better ask up at the lodge."
The message was clear enough: 'piss off'. He looked away to continue talking to his friends who now ignored my presence in a way that emphasized my dismissal from their company.

I was in Swaledale as the result of a phone call made to the London offices of up-market estate agents Strutt and Parker. I knew from reading *The Field* and *The Shooting Times* that

S. & P. ran a leading sporting agency for the letting of fishing and shooting rights. Contacting them had seemed a good way to find a summer job loading on a grouse moor. A loader, in the shooting world, is a person who stands beside the person doing the shooting to load his shotguns. The shooter could of course do this himself but, where large numbers of birds are expected, it is traditional to use two double-barrelled guns to increase firepower. While one gun is being fired the loader loads the other one ready to pass it to the shooter before reloading the empty gun. In modern times it would of course be possible to use a repeating shotgun holding five or more shells but nobody who knows the first thing about it would ever have the nerve to appear on a grouse moor with such an affront to tradition. Occasionally one would appear in the hands of an American, both gun and owner regarded askance. To rent a day or a week on a grouse moor you need a tremendous amount of money, and then another tremendous amount to afford the matched pair of hand-made shotguns to actually shoot the grouse with.

I was only twenty, a little naïve, but enthusiastic about shooting. In much the same way that I thought becoming a rural land agent would give me a back-door entry to the farming world, I surmised loading would be a cheap way of getting onto a grouse moor, even if I would not actually be doing the shooting. Better than cheap because I would be paid, not to mention being in receipt of generous tips from the 'guns' I loaded for. It seemed an interesting way to spend a few weeks cornering some cash. I had not been so naïve in talking to Strutt and Parker as not to stress my upcoming enrolment at the Royal Agricultural College in Cirencester. I realised this information would serve as an indication that I might have the right sort of credentials for the job.

It must have done the trick because someone called me back to say one of their clients, Lord Peel of Carnforth Castle, owned extensive grouse moors in Yorkshire and might well be worth contacting. They had passed on my details he said. Soon after this the phone had rung in my mother's Suffolk bungalow.

"Peel here at Carnforth. Is that Jack?"

"Yes, it is."

"I believe you want to come up for the grouse?"

A brief conversation followed in which we agreed dates and I was promised a confirming letter from the Carnforth estate office setting out terms. What I had not anticipated was that my fellow loaders would all be Old Etonian associates of Peel, an elitist gang resistant, as I was now discovering, to the inclusion of an outsider 'pleb' in their number. A childhood at boarding school inures you to this sort of behaviour but nonetheless the lack of welcome left me feeling apprehensive of the next few weeks

In the last of the daylight I walked up to the lodge, a two-storey stone building on high ground with long views eastwards down Swaledale. It looked quite imposing. I found a service entrance opening onto a corridor. Voices were audible. I shouted 'Hello'. A female voice echoed mine,

"Hello, come through."

The corridor opened into a spacious, warm kitchen where three women and a man sat around a table crowded with plates and bottles. The man, in his late fifties, was smoking, with one leg across his knee and his chair pushed back. It was obvious they had just finished eating; the feeling was one of welcoming ease. The women were all well groomed and attractive, the two younger ones I guessed at about five years older than me. I wondered if the other was the wife of the smoker. As soon as I entered the room the girl sitting at the end of the table leaned forward to pull out a chair and said

"Sit down. Glass of wine?"

"I'd love one." I answered as I did as I had been told. I noticed the wine looked expensive. This was more like it. I told them who I was and related the situation down at the cottage.

"Oh that's no problem," said the girl who had welcomed

me "there're umpteen rooms upstairs all made up ready for odd-bods like you arriving late. You can take your pick."

"Yes," said the second girl "and eat with us here in the kitchen. Breakfast at seven but dinner not until about nine-thirty after the guests have finished. Have you eaten? Would you like something?"

It was now nearly ten o'clock and I hadn't stopped since leaving Suffolk before lunch. As I ate my way through two thick slices of *boeuf en croute* with gravy and vegetables my companions identified themselves. The girls, Charlotte and Amanda, were *Cordon Bleu* qualified, hired up from London as chefs for the lodge. Maggie, the older lady, was acting as sous-chef. The man, Michael, was not her husband but the butler, chauffeur and general assistant over from Carnforth castle for the season. These four, supported by two local housemaids who came in at nine each morning, provided hospitality and housekeeping to the various parties of eight or so 'guns' that arrived every Sunday for a week's shooting.

I learnt that the party just arrived were drawn from German aristocracy: princes, barons and dukes. This prompted some banter as to which of them would fall in love with the girls, though I picked up that as nationalities went the Germans were appreciated for their discipline and good shooting, if not for their relaxed sense of humour. Quite different, they said, from the Italians who were far too excitable and shot at everything including (accidentally) the beaters. Apparently the French were nearly as bad with the added difficulty that it was impossible to get them back out on the moor after lunch. The Americans hadn't a clue but were very friendly, if apt to show up with strange weaponry and fluorescent red caps that scared every grouse for miles. The English were rare- they simply couldn't afford it.

All these people paid huge amounts to shoot the grouse and enjoyed luxury accommodation provided by the lodge. Only the best would do- Scottish beef, wild salmon, lobster, venison and the finest wines. The good thing about this, as I had just discovered, was that an excellent 'trickle-down effect' operated in that the kitchen, now to include me, dined on this same fare each night once the guests had left the dining room. It occurred that I had landed on my feet. Socially speaking Charlotte and Amanda might have been the 'Sloane Ranger' equivalents of the Old Etonians but unlike the latter they were welcoming, beautiful and flirtatious.

I arrived in the kitchen just before 7am to find the team busy with preparations for the day ahead.

"Bacon and eggs?" asked Charlotte

"I couldn't" I said "not after all that food last night. But maybe I could take something for lunch."

"Don't worry," she told me "we'll send something up with Michael."

Strategically located up on the moors were a number of small, stone-built huts. Each contained one room with an open fireplace at a gable end. Furnished with trestle table and benches they provided comfortable respite for the shooters at lunchtimes. As they were sited so as to be accessible by Land Rover Michael was able to drive up well before noon each day to make preparations for the meal. Linen and silverware would be laid, cut glasses polished and a peat fire lit in the grate. When the 'guns' arrived he would continue in butler mode, serving drinks and ladling out the warming stews or casseroles brought up from the lodge in insulated containers. There was nothing very 'picnicky' about these luncheons.

In the damp heather outside the hut it was a different story, if no less hierarchical. The tweed-clad keepers formed one group of perhaps half-a-dozen men. They would sit at some distance from the much larger group of beaters, perhaps twenty persons, young and old, male and female. The loaders, as many as there were 'guns'- usually eight- made up a third group which, again, sat separately from the other two groups. 'Only in England' I thought as I sat down tentatively in the heather at the edge of the loader group. I had exchanged a word or two with a couple of the Etonians during the course of the morning but this had not led to any convivial conversation. Now I was in the embarrassing situation of very obviously not having any lunch as they unwrapped the sandwiches they had made up before leaving their cottage. I was debating whether or not to interrupt Michael in the middle of his ministrations in the hut when he appeared in its doorway with a wicker lunch basket in one hand. He walked over.

"Sorry Jack, I forgot to give you this."

A red-checked gingham cloth covered the contents. These were: a plated, film-wrapped chicken salad; a ramekin of salmon pate, another smaller one of mayonnaise and a third larger one of chocolate mousse. In addition a knife and fork, a linen napkin, a mini-bottle of white wine, a glass and a thermos of coffee. A stillness descended over the Etonians as I laid out this lunch in the heather around me. They, I had noticed, were eating sliced white bread sandwiches filled with what looked like jam. This whole episode greatly strengthened my trust in the principles of Karma.

By the end of September the peak of the shooting was over. The coveys of grouse were beginning to amalgamate into large 'packs' that came over the guns in big 'all or nothing' flocks. Amanda went back to London. A mellow autumnal feel was settling into the dale as the annual lamb sales approached. The prices realised would make or break the year's finances on the small tenant farms.

One evening someone said there was live music on at the pub in Muker. So after dinner Charlotte and I walked the steep mile up to the Farmers' Arms. There had been a big lamb sale over at Hawes during the day. Prices had been good, rents could be paid and the pub was crowded with happy drinkers.

Jammed in a corner three musicians with fiddle, accordion and Irish drum struggled to play over the noise. The door stood open to the cobbled square where a bonfire had been lit to mark the Michaelmas term day. As Charlotte and I walked in a voice roared from the bar.

"Ah! Princess Charlotte, queen of Gunnerside!"
A barrel of a man with a tweed cap twisted askew on top of a red football of a face stepped toward us, threw his arms about our shoulders and shepherded us to the bar. This was 'Big John', the bachelor tenant whose sheep grazed over the moors above us. I had not met him before but had overheard kitchen talk of his immense strength and extraordinary capacity for food and beer. Clearly the day had gone well for John at the auction mart. His arms held our shoulders in a tight squeeze, a manoeuvre that threatened to burst the seams of the thick tweed jacket that wrapped John in an earthy smell of sheep, diesel and beer.

"Now then, you'll have a whisky on me."
It was a statement, not a question. He pushed a fiver across the bar, drained his beer and banged down the glass.

"And then we'll have a dance!"
The prospect seemed a little frightening at first but, as the whisky joined forces with the wine we had drunk with dinner, Dutch courage soon marched to the rescue.

The pub was emptying into the square as people took up positions around the bonfire. The musicians had reassembled on some stools carried out from the bar and struck up a reel. People began stomping around in circles waving glasses above their heads. Charlotte and I were still inside with John when he decided it was time to join them. He stooped forward between us, put an arm around each of our waists and hoisted us from the floor as if we were two lambs. Airborne we were carried out into the square.

At the edge of the fire John made no move to release us. Instead he began to dance. Lifting one knee high and then the other, he began dipping his shoulders to the music, first to the left, then to the right, gathering momentum. Still airborne we rose and dipped with him like evenly balanced counterweights on a human set of scales. Around us figures silhouetted by the fire cavorted in their own wildly improvised moves. Faces glowed red with alcohol and sweat. Towers of sparks soared into the night whenever someone hurled more wood into the fire. The music increased in tempo and John danced ever faster, a partner under each arm. Surrounded by the dark and empty moors we were aloft in the arms of a giant. The fire glowed red hot just beside us. Drunken dancers stamped madly to ever-faster music. I wondered for a moment if we might be suddenly flung into the flames as some primeval sacrifice to the god of sheep. It did not seem too incredible an idea. At last John's exertions so close to the heat required him to recover his pint from inside the pub. He dropped us on our feet. The square spun around me as I struggled to stay upright on the cobbles. Charlotte looked a bit pale.

Back from the bar with a glass of beer in one hand, John put his other hand on his knee and stooped forward to look closely into her face.

"Now then, you've seen I can dance- will you marry me?" Charlotte brought her face nose to nose with John's and knitted her brows into a serious expression.

"Can I think about it John? I'll let you know next season." John straightened up and threw both arms skyward as if offering his beer in a desperate supplication to the gods. Gazing up into the darkness he boomed

"It'll be too late girl, I'll be snapped up in minutes now they've seen my moves! You've lost your chance!" And he moved off to select his next partner from amongst the fire-lit figures.

Walking back down the dale Charlotte seemed unusually pensive. I wondered aloud if she thought she *had* missed her chance.

"Don't be silly" she said. It didn't sound all that convincing.

HARRY

Next door to my mother's bungalow in Suffolk was a smaller, wooden one called The Homestead. In it lived a retired sergeant major named Fred and his wife Claire, a Maltese-Greek he had married in Cairo while on service. With them lived their daughter Antoinette and their son Harry. Actually there wasn't room for Harry so he slept in a caravan at the back.

At 22 Harry was only a year older than me but light years ahead in terms of women, beer and general roust-about experience. He had left school at fifteen for a joinery apprenticeship and now worked as a sub-contract carpenter. He knew every tradesman for miles, every pub and most of the available women. He sometimes emerged from his caravan into the purging sunlight of a Sunday morning proudly exhibiting a black eye, or worse: pub-brawl injuries suffered after deliberately provoking some girl's escort to violence. Harry combined his mother's Mediterranean looks and Latin temperament with the bullish Anglo-Saxon vigour of his father. He was small but tough- he could take a 56lb weight in each hand and with arms straight out from his sides lift both simultaneously to shoulder height and then hoist them straight up above his head. If Harry had a black eye it was likely the other man was still in hospital. Fred was quite proud of him.

For my part I could only just lift one weight with both hands, and then only to waist height. I was spending most of my time away at agricultural college in the Cotswolds with a lot of

Old Etonians and Hooray Henrys. I knew hardly anyone locally, had no idea how to carry on with women and had never been in a fight in all my adult life. A pint of lager made me dizzy. But Harry and I got on famously. Mainly this was because we were both enthusiastic about the traditional sport of the Suffolk coast- wildfowling and shooting. We had shared the cost of a small dinghy to take us up and down the Alde estuary in pursuit of the wintering flocks of wigeon and mallard. It was only ten feet long, a rotting clinker-built thing, but it did allow us access to the tidal foreshore of all the big shooting estates along the river up to Snape and down to Orford. The theory was that as long as we were below the high-water mark we were not trespassing, although the gamekeepers that pursued us seemed deaf to the legalities.

A particularly touchy location was Ham Creek just upstream from the spot known locally as 'Little Japan'. Little Japan because a row of twisted pines lined a low cliff above a sandy beach, giving a vaguely oriental look to the landscape. The touchiness because Ham Creek lay directly beneath the flight line of ducks moving between the tidal estuary and the Blackheath estate's main decoy pond. Fred Keeble, the estate's gamekeeper, kept the decoy fed with barley to attract ducks for the sporting recreation of the gentry. Sitting in our dinghy in Ham creek one winter afternoon we fired a couple of shots at a flight of inbound mallard, thereby alerting Fred to our presence. It wasn't long before we heard his old Land Rover grinding along the track below the far side of the river wall. It stopped and Fred, gun under his arm, appeared on top of the wall. He was accompanied by two large Alsatian dogs- not a usual breed for gamekeepers but one Fred found effective for discouraging nocturnal pheasant poachers.

"Goo on, sod orf out of it!" he shouted down to us.
We waved back cheerfully. Harry shouted "A'ternoon Fred." We knew him from previous encounters.

"You boys set foot on them saltings these here dawgs 'll rip yer arses orf!" We waved again. Our insolence didn't improve

Fred's temper.

"If'n I put a hole just on the waterline o' that ole tub you cocky buggers'll ha' ter come ashore. Lest y're bloody gud swimmers. Then the dawgs 'll get yer!"

He raised his gun in our direction. We waved again but then I unshipped the oars to move and Fred lowered the gun to watch us row away.

"What did you do that for?" said Harry. Backing down was not something he approved of.

"Didn't like the look of those Alsatians" I answered.

"Fuck's sake" said Harry "we're armed aren't we?"

"So was Fred" I said, "shoot his dogs he might have got proper upset."

"Bastard!" Harry concluded.

Once we heard the Land Rover chug away we rowed back to where we'd been.

*   *   *

In 1970 I came home for the Christmas break to find Harry was working on concrete shuttering for the planned Sizewell B nuclear power station*. The weather was severe with a strong easterly gale threatening snow, ideal for wildfowling. I agreed to meet Harry at Sizewell at 3pm to give us time to get up the river in time for the evening flight.

"Did you get the oars?" said Harry as I put my gun and waterproofs into his battered ex. Post Office van.

The original red livery had been painted over by hand in a dirty yellow.

"I thought you'd got them in here" I answered.

"Dipshit" said Harry "I told you I'd taken them out to repair!"

I remembered I was supposed to have collected them from the house in Saxmundham where Harry now lived with his girl-friend. We could either abort the trip or make a dash for the oars, in which case it was doubtful we would have time to get in position on the river before dark. We went for the oars.

Never during or after its official duties had the Morris

been driven as Harry now drove it. Screeching through the narrow S-bends on the Saxmundham road it seemed certain the tyres would burst or the wheels come off or the engine seize, or all of these, but I knew Harry better than to attempt a calming word. It would have only poured petrol on the flames. Hunched forward over the wheel, silent and grim in concentration, he kept his foot to the floor, willing the old vehicle to greater speed.

Arriving at the one set of traffic lights in the town we ignored the red and swung into the High Street drawing indignant looks from shoppers as we accelerated along its length. We skidded left into the narrow lane servicing the rear of the shops. Harry's girlfriend's house fronted onto this lane at its far end. Too far, because filling the lane from wall to wall was a large lorry approaching at a crawl. It stopped and the driver jumped down from the cab to make a delivery. This was too much for Harry. From behind the windscreen he delivered a tirade of unjustified abuse at the innocent driver who, sensing our displeasure, gave us an indifferent look and carried on with his delivery.

Harry crashed the gearbox into reverse, floored the accelerator and popped the clutch. This was too much for the Morris. An acrid smell of scorched rubber rose from its tyres as all visibility vanished under a spreading cumulus of steam pouring from its front end. Not letting up on the expletives Harry leapt from the driver's seat and threw open the bonnet. Under the pressure of rally-style driving a radiator hose had blown off. Harry grabbed a large screwdriver from the van and jammed the hose back on. He was beginning to tighten the jubilee clip when it blew off again and shot a jet of steam into his face. This was nearly the end as far as Harry was concerned. Like some demented murderer he raised the screwdriver high above the engine block and began repeatedly stabbing at it while screaming insults at the inanimate machine, its human manufacturers and the world in general. An elderly couple carrying shopping bags watched open-mouthed before hurrying off, fearful the target off Harry's rage might widen to include bystanders. The lorry driver, now back in his cab, held a 'what-a-prat' grin as he waited for us to move out of his way.

All these people must have felt a sense of *deja-vu* when some years later John Cleese performed a similar attack on his car in a famous episode of *Fawlty Towers*. Harry's version was a lot darker, there was no humour and the expletives could never have been broadcast.

After Harry and the Morris returned to what passed as normal functioning we arrived at Slaughden quay with the oars but without time to get in position before dark. Had we been sensible we would have abandoned the attempt there and then but we were not, and besides, we had gone through hell to get where we were. We tipped the water and ice out of our little wooden dinghy and the three of us (Harry's dog Bruno was the third) pushed off, having agreed we would land on the nearest bit of salting on the far shore instead of trying to get further up-river. The tide was ebbing strongly against the continuing easterly gale. This set up a nasty chop that soon had Harry baling as I rowed.

The estuary here is wide and bends a bit so going in the desired direction while facing backwards in the near dark in a gale is challenging. Unhelpfully Harry kept shouting contradictory instructions. Then the edge of some saltings appeared in front of us. Just as we prepared to land we recognised we were still on the Slaughden side of the river. This was hopeless because the Aldeburgh gunners almost continuously manned these marshes, scaring away all the duck. Reaching undisturbed shores had been our whole point in getting the boat. At this point Bruno, seeing dry land close at hand, and possibly by now seasick, made a leap for it and splashed ashore. Getting him back into the boat nearly capsized it and further excited Harry.

After a hard row in the increasing dark we got ashore in what we thought was a better place. We loaded our guns and waited in the ridiculous optimism that if anything flew right over us we might have been able to see it. In fact if anything had actually flown right *into* us it was unlikely we would have seen it. After half an hour or so we got back in the boat and headed home in defeat. Except we had no idea in which direction to head. According to Harry I was rowing in circles. That was quite possible given the dark and the conditions. Then it began to snow hard, the wind-driven blizzard reducing visibility to nothing at all. This was no joke as the ebb was sweeping us downriver at speed and Harry's baling was failing to keep pace with the rising water level inside the boat. Then the oars hit the soft mud of a shoreline. Happy to accept any fate other than drowning we jumped out into the slime and freezing water. We leaned down hard on the transom, skimmed the boat up to dry land and set off walking in the hope of discovering where we were. After a few minutes Slaughden quay loomed out of the darkness, our first stroke of luck that afternoon.

While I remarked on my skills at nocturnal navigation Harry repeatedly pushed the starter button on the Morris. It was no good; the battery was dying, then dead. The snow and the cold were too much for it. But no matter, this was an old vehicle that came equipped with a crank starter. Harry, got out, unshipped the handle, inserted it and started cranking. I sat in the passenger seat sheltering from the blast. The engine fired suddenly but died immediately and then there was Harry leaping around in the dark nursing his wrist and swearing again. The Morris had mounted a counter-attack, kicking back the crank to add injury to the list of persecutions Harry faced. He had dropped the crank handle but now picked it up and began beating the bonnet of the Morris in an even fiercer repetition of the High Street attack. Cowering in the cab I watched as he reduced the smooth curve of the bonnet to a range of undulating foothills rising to the windscreen. I was afraid that might be next.

The snow continued to fall relentlessly on this scene of human and mechanical frailty. Its effect was to provide a surreal, almost pantomime, quality to the moment. Nonetheless, safely back at home, I felt lucky to have got away with my life.

* This was when the CEGB thought they might just get on and build it without too much ado. Later the project was put on hold pending a public inquiry.

REVENGE OF THE PIG

Most post-war baby boomers complain that the adventure has gone out of travel thanks to the internet. 'Traveller' has become synonymous with 'tourist'. Fancy a trip to Ulan Bator? Spend half an hour logged on to booking.com or trivago and you can book every detail, complete with bird's eye and street level views of your accommodation. Once you're there your smartphone can instantly flash videos of local colour to the 'devices' of friends and family, never mind they might be watching in a jam on the M25 or on top of a bus in Streatham.

It never used to be like this: you had to work at travel. Bookings were not instantly available. Information was hard to obtain and often unreliable. Travel guides had to be consulted. Letters had to be written and received, cheques posted and acknowledged. All time-consuming and tedious perhaps, but the absence of immediate communication meant that a large element of what eventually happened to you was down to luck and circumstance. Particularly so if you were young and travelling on little more than hope, charity and a sense of adventure. Destinations were chosen on nothing more than hearsay or some tenuous foreign contact. And reporting the experience was limited to what might fit on an occasional postcard home and the few Instamatic snaps not thrown away on collection from the chemist because light or water had got into the camera.

Now, despite the Brexit debacle, my children consider travel anywhere in Europe as being just a bit further on than

Bournemouth. They see Corsica as no more than a popular destination for package deals. But in 1970 we regarded that island more warily as the home of a violent campaign for independence from France; a mountainous refuge for fiery Franco-Italian bandits for whom blowing up banks and assassinating politicians was a way of life. That all tended to discourage tourists, so by definition making Corsica an interesting, almost exotic, destination. And crucially, being in Europe, it was cheap to get to. You could get a stand-by flight from London to Marseilles for £10 one-way. From Marseilles or Nice a ferry ran to Ajaccio or Calvi costing foot passengers only a few francs.

Hard to believe now but back then you could take the flight to Marseilles armed with an assortment of weaponry. Admittedly my rifle was inside a backpack with only the barrel protruding from the top, but nonetheless it was obviously a rifle barrel and not a tent pole. In full view, on the other hand, was the razor-sharp, three-pronged spear gun that, being too long to check in, I was told to carry on board as hand luggage. Of course at the time, apart from the bombing campaigns of a couple of world wars, not much had happened by way of airborne terrorism. Some rogue Cubans had hijacked a handful of planes in America but metal detectors and armed security at airports were unimagined developments for the future.

The purpose of taking a spear gun to the Mediterranean is self-evident but the rifle requires explanation. As an avid consumer of the writings of Hemingway and Thoreau I knew, that had those famous outdoorsmen been going camping in wild Corsica, they would have lived off the land: spearing fish in the sea, catching trout from the mountain streams and shooting wild boar in the *maquis* scrub. So of course I would do the same. Chris and Philip, my two companions from agricultural college, if not completely in thrall to the same ideals, were all in favour of the potential budget savings. Our plan, such as it was, was to spend a few days snorkelling on the beaches while living on speared fish before heading up into the inland mountains in search of wild pigs to barbecue. But before leaving the coast it was obvious a little insider knowledge would be a good idea.

The current tourist era may have provoked greater affability in the Corsican population but in 1970 they were a taciturn lot. If not actually hostile to strangers they were not particularly welcoming either. If you did manage to engage someone in conversation chances were he or she would be speaking an Italian-French patois that bore very little relation to inadequate schoolboy French. Help came, surprisingly, from the intercession of the police.

Under normal circumstances we took care to maintain as low a profile as possible when in view of the *gendarmerie.* Not that we ever had any evil intent, more a precautionary principle in case we were inadvertently violating some arcane local byelaw. Surprisingly, given the situation on the beaches of the nearby *Cote d' Azur,* one such Corsican byelaw banned topless sunbathing, at least if you were female. Enforcing this statute must have been a popular assignment as it demanded patrolling the beach to advise those found flouting the law to cover up.

One searingly hot afternoon the attention of the patrolling officer was diverted from breast duty by the sight of the rifle lying inside our open tent. Seeing a chance to avert violent crime as perhaps a worthwhile alternative to eliminating bronzed boobs, he approached to make enquiries. A disjointed explanation of our non-criminal intentions followed. It was not difficult to convince him of our innocence, clearly we were not the hard men of a hit squad.

Unfortunately this officer knew nothing of pigs or hunting but he said he knew a man who would. On a page of a small official notebook, no doubt useful for recording the details of recalcitrant sunbathers, he wrote down an address in central Ajaccio. Tearing off this page he handed it to me before leaving with an air of disappointment at not having foiled a coup or assassination. Yet it was difficult to feel any sympathy as he strolled away in search of the next young beauty innocently offending the law.

At the address I had been given a brass plate identified the building as a government office, in particular the workplace of *le Directeur du Chasse Corse*. Presumably as a civil servant *le directeur* would at least speak an identifiable French. There was no bell so I tried the handle of the heavy wooden door. It let me into the dim light of a surprisingly cool anteroom. A smartly dressed woman looked up from a desk.

"*Bonjour*"

"*Bonjour. Le directeur du chasse, il est ici?*"

"*Oui*"

In my stumbling French of few phrases and poorly conjugated verbs I attempted to explain the reason for my presence in her office. She rose from her desk and moved to a door at the rear of the room. Knocking lightly she leant around it to speak to the occupant, presumably *le directeur*. She pushed the door open, beckoned me forward, and shut the door behind me.

A balding man of about fifty in sand-coloured fatigues sat in a swivel chair pushed back from a large, heavy desk. A pointer dog underneath it raised its head inquisitively at my entry. Seeing nothing of interest it went back to sleep. The man, the desk, myself and everything else appeared to be under a camouflage net created by thin bars of horizontal sunlight penetrating the venetian blinds. It was as if we were all in a scene from an art-house movie. *Le directeur* was resting one ankle on a knee and held a cup of coffee in his lap. He appeared extremely relaxed.

"*Bonjour*"

"*Bonjour Monsieur*"

I repeated the explanation I had given his secretary, finishing by asking if it would be in order for me to shoot one of his pigs.

"*C'est possible?*"

"*D'accord*"

I continued by asking where I would find the wild pigs, *les sangliers*.

"*Dans le foret, le maquis, les champs, partout!*" he said, waving a free hand expansively as if indicating the whole of the island. "*Mais cherchez les arbres de figue, le figue sauvage. Avant l'aube, tres tot le matin.*"

It seemed the pigs were very partial to wild figs at first light. I thanked him as best I could for this encouraging advice, and left his office a little surprised that apparently I needed no sort of licence or authorising paperwork. Refreshingly 'wild west'. What he really thought of an idiotic young Englishman chasing about the island with a rifle he had been too polite to let show.

Fired with enthusiasm for *la chasse* after this brief interview, I chivvied the others to leave our beach encampment for the interior.

"It will be lovely and cool up in the mountains. Clear streams and lakes to swim in. Bracing air, and think of the sizzling pork chops over the campfire."

I must have sounded persuasive because we agreed to decamp and hitchhike independently to the remote village of Soccia in the high mountains fifty miles north of Ajaccio. There we would meet up before making the steep climb up to the basin of the Lac de Nino where, for no other reason than its remoteness, I was confident we would find abundant wild figs and pigs.

In 1970 Soccia may have been untouched by tourism but it was about to receive the very latest in German engineering in the form of two new Bosch washing machines. I knew this because the plumber delivering them from Ajaccio gave me a lift. I guessed that what lay behind his benevolence was the thought that I might come in useful once we arrived in Soccia. A medieval mountain village of terraced streets, perpendicular steps and narrow alleys impassable to vehicles makes the delivery of white goods a challenging proposition. What he hadn't perhaps calculated was that the addition of the modest weight of me and my backpack would constitute the straw that would threaten to break the back of his 150cc Piaggio three-wheeler van, already taxed to the limit by the two washing machines.

All was well for the first few miles of relatively gentle inclines but once into the mountains proper things went downhill fast but uphill at no more than walking pace, accompanied by the dying whine of a two-stroke engine pushed beyond its design targets. This didn't seem to worry the heavily stubbled plumber Paolo, who, I sensed, might be accustomed to testing most things to destruction. As we negotiated each crucifying hairpin he only grinned and laughed at the impossibility of the next stretch of near vertical road appearing in front of us. He put me in mind of a sadist relishing the weakening screams of a victim. On the final precipitous approach to Soccia I got out and walked alongside. This was actually a relief as it was easy to imagine the little Piaggio sliding backwards out of control and disappearing off the side of the road into the adjoining gorge, taking Paolo and the German machines with it.

Our arrival caused great excitement amongst the women of the village. This is not a sexist comment because it was a fact that there were no men visible anywhere. Perhaps they had seen us coming and instinctively remembered there were urgent tasks elsewhere precluding the handling of washing machines. Maybe Paolo had had previous experience of male absenteeism because his forethought in giving me a lift now paid off. We humped and heaved the first Bosch from the back of the Piaggio. A cobbled alley and a series of low stone steps lay between us and its final destination. He had brought a wheeled sack barrow to help but given the uneven terrain it was of no use, threatening to shake the Bosch apart. Attended by half a dozen chattering ladies dressed in black, and with minimal clearance in any direction, we fought the machine up the steps and into the new owner's house.

After the scorching sunlight outside it was comfortably dark and cool. A large crucifix gleaming palely from one wall. Paolo stripped away the packing from the machine as the ladies stood by admiringly, occasionally bending forward to examine its controls. All but the new owner and her daughter (or it might have been her daughter-in-law, I couldn't catch it) then filed out leaving the white cube of the Bosch squat and square in the middle of the room, its shiny technology looking very out of place amongst simple furnishings probably unchanged for generations. Another struggle got it through a doorway into a kitchen area at the rear. At which point the two ladies of the house instructed us to sit down for a breather and refreshment.

Although I had a very basic command of French that had allowed me to converse in simple terms with Paolo, his language since arriving in Soccia had switched to the Italian-French patois that left me entirely alienated. I was struggling to decipher gestures and looks and guessing at the rest. There had been a lot of laughter and quick glances in my direction that I hoped had been good-natured, after all I was doing my best to help.

The ladies now brought out a board loaded with bread, salami and cheese, accompanied by a large bottle of red wine and a smaller one of clear liquid, apparently homemade pear brandy. This they insisted we taste first from small shot glasses. It went straight to my head, despite the accompanying food. Paolo was chattering away as he ate and drank, occasionally interpreting into French for my benefit. Eventually he stood up and said he would have to get on with connecting the washing machine. I asked if he wanted me to hang on to give him a hand with the delivery of the second Bosch. 'No, no', he told me, 'these ladies have said the people are not at home, they are staying with their son in Bastia'. I wondered what he would do? 'Oh, take it back to Ajaccio and come back another time'. He was very relaxed about having almost exploded the Piaggio hauling the machine from sea level to over 1000 metres to no purpose. Thanking everyone for all their help and hospitality I exited back out into the sunshine and walked off to look for some cool shade to soften the throbbing in my head.

I had been feeling rather pleased with myself all morning for having managed to get all the way to Soccia with a single lift from Ajaccio. I anticipated a long wait, possibly overnight, for Chris and Philip to catch up. Arriving at the village square I found them waiting for me. They had zoomed up the mountains in the back of a large and comfortable Citroen saloon belonging to a doctor called to a Soccia patient. They were sitting in the shade of the ancient communal *lavoir,* or laundry place. The irony of the location wasn't lost on me.

We camped overnight just outside the village with our plan to make the long climb up to the lake the following day in jeopardy. We had expected to re-provision in Soccia. This had proved impossible, as there was no *epicerie, boulangerie*, nor even a *bar-tabac*. Apparently the residents all drove down the mountain to the shops or else received pre-arranged deliveries. This left us with inadequate food supplies for the four or five day excursion into the high mountains we had vaguely thought about. We had some smelly cheese, some stale bread, a few beef-steak tomatoes and a very fat Corsican-style salami. We could either abandon the whole idea or simply go for one night at the lake and come down again. We set off for the lake. I was very sanguine about the prospects for making it a longer trip.

"Don't worry," I said, "we'll shoot a pig and have enough food for a month."

"Have you seen a pig anywhere in Corsica yet?" asked Philip

"No but we haven't got to the land where the fig tree grows."

"Where in a wood a piggy wig stood," added Chris, taking the cue.

"Exactly. Plus I bet the lake is full of trout. No worries at all."

Philip was not convinced:

"That's what Captain Scott said when he set off."

"What, that the fishing prospects were good?"

He didn't answer.

"Anyway that was 40 below, this is 40 above."

This was true because although still quite early the temperature was climbing as steeply as the path. We lapsed into a sweaty silence.

Three hours or so later we had somehow lost the path as we climbed toward a ridge through the *maquis*. The *maquis* or, less romantically, scrub of the south of France, and particularly of Corsica, is famous for its fragrant blend of wild herbs and flowers. It's probably at its best in spring. By August it's not so much fragrant as scratchy, in places downright thorny, and in places dense enough to be impenetrable. Here it was growing on a steep terrain of rock and sand that would have been hard enough going on a cloudy day of cool breezes. Under cloudless blue at the height of a Mediterranean summer it was enough to bring us to our knees.

Actually Philip was already on his knees a few metres above me when he turned to hiss down "Pig!" before putting a finger in front of his mouth to signal silence. With the index finger of his other hand he pointed upwards with a sort of tapping motion.

"Quick, bring the rifle" he mouthed.
I hurriedly assembled the gun and as quietly and quickly as I could scrambled up to Philip. I could hear gently grunting pig noises above us.

"It's just over these rocks" whispered Philip "a big one on its own. I don't think it saw me."
I inched up towards the contented sound of a snuffling pig. Philip came up beside me as I eased the rifle to the lip of the rocks and peeked over. There, rooting about in a patch of *maquis*, was an enormous white sow.

"That's not a wild boar"
"Of course it is! Shoot it!"
"That's a domestic pig"
"What's it doing up here then"
"I dunno, but I'm not going to shoot it."
At which point we both stood up. The pig, probably alerted by the sudden whiff of human sweat, stared at us momentarily with a surprised expression before trotting briskly off.

"There goes dinner," said Philip
"Wild pigs are small and black" I told him "that belonged to someone."

Our appetites stimulated we broke for lunch and managed to consume most of our supplies, only by huge force of will saving the big *saucisson* for dinner.

We returned to the ascent and soon discovered the lucky

wisdom of our clemency toward the pig. Cresting a ridge we found ourselves looking down on the blue circle of le Lac de Nino. Circumscribing it was a level expanse of velvety-looking grass on which grazed ponies, cows and several dozen large white sows identical to, and probably now including, the one we had nearly ambushed. Herding them from a tented encampment at the near end of the lake we could see figures tending fires and unsaddling horses. These we were sure were indigenous Corsican bandits whose day would have been made by spit-roasting three Brits who had dared to murder one of their pigs.

With a few hours of daylight left we decided to head for high ground above the far end of the lake. The lake itself looked too shallow to be very 'trouty' and did not inspire much confidence as a source of food. Hopefully the saddle at its far end would give us an aspect into the next valley where there might be wild pigs as opposed to tame ones. The distance would also provide us with a buffer zone against the graziers who, for obvious reasons, we were anxious not to upset. Hopefully the more distant a rifle shot the less likely they would be to misinterpret its meaning.

We trekked around the edge of the basin to avoid the numerous creeks and springs surrounding the lake. From the saddle a path led down towards an area sparsely wooded with pine that, apart from looking more 'piggy', would give more shelter for a camp than the rocky, alpine area above. But before losing any altitude and visibility Chris and I decided it would be sensible to climb a nearby knoll to get a better idea of the lie of the land below us.

Leaving Philip sitting on top of a boulder at the side of the trail we dropped our packs and set off to climb to this vantage point two hundred yards or so away. We had just achieved it when a series of loud cries came from the trees below. Not cries of alarm but a sort of fragmented yodel. It stopped but a moment or two later started again. A donkey carrying a heavily bearded rider appeared labouring up the trail. In one hand the man held the donkey's halter rope, with the other he scattered something from side to side across the path. It looked like grain maize. He reached into saddlebags slung across the donkey's withers and threw out another handful. Behind him followed a growing column of pigs, identical to the one we might have shot, each stopping briefly to guzzle the grain before trotting quickly on in pursuit of the donkey. As we watched more and more white pigs came trotting hurriedly through the trees to join up behind this Pied Piper.

The donkey had now drawn level with Philip but did not pause. As it passed its rider made no visual sign of acknowledgement that we could see. What we could see from our elevated position was that one of the forward pigs in the column had diverted from the track to the back of the rock propping up our rucksacks. Philip, gazing at the pigs passing in front of him, remained oblivious to this threat. The pig's nose was raised inquisitively as it sniffed hard, homing in on the side pocket of my pack. Therein rested our only remaining food, the fat salami. Realising what was about to happen Chris and I yelled a warning to Philip and raced downhill, but too late. The pig's jaws closed on the pocket of the rucksack. Finding the source of the alluring smell not readily forthcoming it shook the rucksack like a terrier with a rat, oblivious to our booted kicks to its head and rear-end. Then, partially satisfied by a mouthful of crushed salami and torn nylon, it decided the prize wasn't worth the aggravation and trotted off to catch up with its fellows.

Analysis of the damage indicated that the heat of the day had dissolved the grease of the salami, converting the skin into a fat-filled balloon that had exploded under the pig's attack. Apart from the destruction of our meagre dinner this attack had also succeeded in turning my rucksack and everything in it into a tattered collection of oily rags.

"Bloody hell" was all I could manage. Chris was more reflective,

"I wonder if that pig realised that salami might have once been its mate?"

"I don't think it cared," said Philip.

At this point my enthusiasm for hunting down more pig fat collapsed.

After a hungry night and breakfast-less morning we arrived back at our starting point in Soccia, any slight feeling of defeat overwhelmed by stronger sensations of hunger. Together we managed to thumb a lift in the back of a pickup to the nearest bar in Guagno-les-Bains. Coffee and fresh croissants never tasted so good. Especially croissants filled with Parma ham.

LENTRAN

F ive miles west of Inverness on the southern shore of the Moray Firth is Lentran House. Built in 1886 in the grandiose style known as Scottish Baronial it was home to the Inverness city provost before being requisitioned by the RAF during the Second World War. By the time it came on to the open market in the 1960s it was desperately in need of some sympathetic care. It didn't get any.

The buyer was Dick West from Tarporley in Cheshire. West owned racehorses, a property company, a big green Bentley, and a fruit farming business. He was not so much interested in Lentran House as the land that went with it, about a hundred acres looking north over the Firth to the Black Isle. He was happy to take long odds on the old mansion coming good in time but meanwhile the fields sloping down to the sea were a sure bet for growing raspberries. Scotland has long been known for its raspberries- they like the cool, damp climate- but West had a new idea. Most Scottish growers produced fruit for processing into pulp for manufacturing jam. Lentran would supply the English retail market with high quality frozen berries.

Mr West was not a loud or aggressive man. In fact for all his success in business he could be quite diffident. I had met him in 1968 at Gunnerside in Swaledale when I was appointed his 'loader' for a week of grouse shooting. At nine o'clock on the Monday morning I had been unable to find him. The main group of 'guns' were socialising noisily in front of the lodge when I spotted someone in shooting togs hovering at the far end of the terrace. I walked over.

"Are you Mr West?"

"Yes I am," he replied, "good morning. Am I in the right place?"

Through the course of the week I found him affable and courteous. Once it came to light that I was at agricultural college he made the reasonable but unwarranted assumption that I knew something about farming. He recruited me to work at Lentran the following summer. Terms were to be £50 a week all found, which was an offer I couldn't refuse. When it came to it a year later it was all too obvious that, rather than any agricultural knowledge, the essential asset was an ability to get on passably with a very diverse collection of people.

I was told that my job would be to take charge of the freezing operation. This made me supervising foreman of six male New Zealanders and a fluctuating gang of eight or so local women recruited from the Kessock Ferry council estate in Inverness. The Kiwis had been recruited through an agricultural employment agency. Not one of them was under six-foot or over thirty. All of them played hard rugby, could shear two hundred sheep a day and looked as if they probably had two for breakfast each morning.

The women were just as tough if more varied in shape and age. One had arms severely decorated with the scars of self-harm in all stages from bloody to healed. This evidence of mental illness won her no sympathy from her workmates.

"Dae yee nae ken hen yeed die quicker if yee took the knife to yee throat?"

This sort of thing may have been a kind of reverse supportive therapy but I was never sure. Although Kiwis and Scots theoretically spoke the same language neither could understand the other. Both must have found being made subject to the direction of a diminutive Englishman as ludicrous as I did.

Further problems of communication were widespread amongst the several hundred pickers camped out in the raspberry fields. These represented most of the nations of Europe plus Israel and, surprisingly, Egypt. The majority were students recruited through agencies specialising in agricultural workers. Some had a few words of English but this was of limited value when it came to understanding instructions issued in the regional dialect of Hamish, the Scots farm manager, or Archie, the Brummy field supervisor. The scope for misunderstandings was immense. Failures of communication were often compounded by international tensions, most obviously Arab and Israeli ones. The agency that sent these two groups of young people to the same farm either optimistically hoped for brotherhood through shared work experience or else was completely ignorant of twentieth century history. The extent of the agricultural experience of the main workforce was betrayed by the sound of Archie striding up and down the rows of raspberries bellowing in the tones of middle England:

"Just pick the red ones, not the green ones!"

Everybody's fortunes depended on the weather. If it was good even the pickers could make a few pounds by working flat out from dawn to dark. If it was bad the quality of the fruit suffered, picking time was restricted and everyone became depressed. If it was really bad the viability of the whole operation would be called into question and deputations of pickers would march on the office demanding repatriation at the company's expense. They had a point because the piece work rates were set so low that only by working like a manic robot day after day could a person make enough to buy a bus ticket for any destination beyond Inverness. In many cases the students had borrowed the money to travel to Scotland on the strength of anticipated earnings that failed to materialise.

Some individuals, feeling cheated, attempted to improve their financial situation by increasing their picking output in innovative ways. Punnets, ostensibly full of raspberries, would be found to have only a thin surface veneer of fruit over compacted bracken or grass with a stone or two added to fool the field supervisor at weigh-in. Very occasionally much worse substances were used as makeweight. As we had been blast-freezing a percentage of punnets 'as picked' for onward distribution to our less fastidious customers such contaminations made this practice too risky. We concentrated instead on individually quick frozen (IQF) berries.

To freeze the raspberries quickly and individually they were tipped onto a conveyor belt and sprayed with liquid nitrogen. It was a relatively slow and expensive business but it did result in a good product and, importantly, allowed any unwanted material to be removed before it reached the customer. It also meant we couldn't go home until the last raspberry from the day's pick was frozen. As the students did not usually get going until mid-morning and often worked into the evening, the Kiwis and I were frequently still at work in the early hours. On warm and windless nights an unexpectedly peaceful, almost magical, aura could sometimes envelop these late shifts as the creaking conveyor ceaselessly trundled its narrow carpet of raspberries into the freezing plant. We were of course a long way north and in July the time between twilight and dawn barely deserved the description of night. In the near distance the unrippled waters of the Firth lay silvered by moonlight while, on its far side, fields of yellow barley stood clearly visible on the slopes of the Black Isle.

Once the last tray of raspberries was tipped and frozen we could go home to bed. Yet often we did not. If midnight was not too far behind us we knew the students would still be circled around the campfires drinking beer and strumming guitars. Some of them were very pretty, the memory of them releasing sufficient energy to propel us up to the campsite for an hour or so of socialising. This could push bedtime forward to dawn. The Kiwis thrived on this self-inflicted punishment, mainly because they did not have to clock on back at the freezer until 10am when the first raspberries appeared from the fields. But the foreman needed to be on site two hours earlier to get things organised for the new day. After a week of only three hours in bed each night I craved sleep.   My best hope was rain. Rain would stop or slow down picking and so allow an early night. If it rained for a whole day I would sleep. If it rained for a second day I would walk up into the hills behind Lentran and fish for trout. There was however one daily timing never open to variation. Helen Munro, the lovely landlady of our 'digs', served our 'tea' at 6pm on the dot and brooked no latecomers.

The Kiwis were equally determined sticklers for timing on the related matter of pre-prandial refreshment. The five-minute drive from Lentran to Helen's council house in Kirkhill took us past the Bog Roy Inn. We would leave the farm at 5.30 to be at the bar of the Bog Roy at 5.35 with beers in hand by 5.40. So far so good but there is an inviolable New Zealand custom that nobody leaves the bar until each member of the party has called and paid for his 'shout'. That meant six pints each, or in my case three, because being only half the size of the Kiwis I claimed a half-pint handicap on each round. You might think here that it's impossible to drink six pints in twenty minutes. Not so if you are a Kiwi sheep shearer with years of practice at the 'six o'clock swill' behind you*. The session would end with the New Zealanders agitating for a speedy departure to avoid Helen's wrath. In their way would be me standing with five full half-pints still lined up on the bar. I would be finishing my first.

"Dammit, we'll be late for Helen. Drink up!"

"C'mon you bastards, you know I can't drink all this."

"Jeez, I guess we'll have to help you out again Half-Pint."
And with that each of the five Kiwis would pick up one of the full glasses and drain it as if it were a thimble of water. We would sit down at Helen's kitchen table with seconds to spare as she handed out plates of mince and tatties. After our first stop at the Bog Roy it was inevitable I would be known ever afterwards as 'Half-Pint'.

◆ ◆ ◆

Apart from the more or less divine intervention of rain there was a more prosaic development that could halt production: strike action by the student pickers. Any potential militant training for a career in the trade unions could find fertile ground on the campsite. At least once during the season some firebrand would motivate a general strike throughout the entire workforce. This was no mean achievement given its size, disparate nature and various language barriers. The students had my sympathy, for at the piecework rate of two pence for each 16oz punnet picked, only the most determined and efficient could hope to make more than the train fare home.

These lowly picking rates would be agreed between Dick West and the one other grower in our area before the season began. The collaboration was designed to implement a uniformity of pay that would prevent his poaching our workers. As we had a hold over the man, in that we froze and marketed his fruit, it seemed unlikely he would break ranks. But harvesting panics are integral to fruit growing and the Scottish weather can reduce windows of opportunity to tiny portholes. Suddenly a rumour flared that this other farm, about eight miles west of us, was paying *three* pence per punnet. Columns of hitchhiking students appeared on the road out of Lentran. West telephoned the grower and refused to handle his fruit. Whole contingents of revolting students were sacked *en masse*. A deputation of French pickers marched on the office waving signs demanding more pay and, receiving no sympathy, upheld the pyrotechnic traditions of French activists by setting fire to the large marquee that served as a communal mess tent. A group of Egyptian students ran amok in Inverness after attempting to drown their sorrows in alcohol, to which they were unaccustomed, and these had to be retrieved from the main police station after midnight. Such entertainments broke the monotony of freezing raspberries day after day.

Occasionally I would be required to drive over to Dalcross to check on a packing operation we had contracted out to a company located on the industrial estate adjoining Inverness airport. Boxes of frozen raspberries were tipped onto a stainless steel table to allow the best and largest to be selected by hand and placed into Marks & Spencer packaging. In the berry sector at least that firm's reputation for quality was justified.

Food processing dominated this part of the site, bathing it with the salty tang of a fish market. Next to our raspberry packing shed was a building in which prawns and shrimp were mechanically peeled before freezing. Opposite was a plate-freezing plant into which daily flowed a shining stream of slip-pery mackerel, brought by lorry from the western ports. Twice a week this flow was interrupted by the arrival of a flatbed truck loaded with steel milk churns from a nearby slaughterhouse. The churns were full of blood, miscellaneous bits of offal and general gunge. Two men in rubber thigh boots pulled off the lids and poured the frothing, fermenting mix of gore into the plate freezers. It splashed over them and then spilled in a dripping, coagulating mess from the bed of the lorry to run across the concrete and threaten the prawn factory. By the time the churns were empty the men could have been taken for the filthy sur-vivors of some awful medieval battle. An hour or two later the blood emerged from the plates as solid, pallet-sized slabs ready for processing into black pudding. I never could eat the stuff.

By the end of the first week in August it was all over, the raspberries picked and frozen, the students dispersed and the money made. I woke up as usual at Helen's, realised my time was my own and fell back on the pillow. I listened to the throaty orchestra of the wood pigeons. Hundreds were concealed in the summer-heavy foliage of the trees that lined the cornfields spread along the shore of the Firth. I remembered happily how much I had put in my bulging wallet. I was due to report to the grouse moors in a week or so but in the meantime I had wheels and money and I could roam the Highlands at will, seeking out friends and adventures. At twenty-two it didn't seem as if it could get much better. And the early 1970s was a good time to be in the Highlands.

It was a boom time. Every year the condensed energy of the short Highland summer creates that feeling; a brief season of long, mild days bringing tourists from around the world flocking to Skye and Inverness, the industry that depends on them shifting into top gear. But in the '70s Inverness felt like a frontier town because other, much bigger excitements were afoot. Extensive oilfields had been discovered in the North Sea and the rush was on to exploit them. A shipyard for the construction of huge oil platforms was building just north of Lentran at Nigg Bay. Oil workers from around the world were squeezing out the tourists from hotels and boarding houses. The fishing was also on a roll with fleets of East European 'Klondykers' anchored off Ullapool buying and processing Scottish mackerel. Their crews would run ashore in 'liberty launches', clean out Ullapool's small stock of consumer luxuries and catch the morning bus to Inverness. The return run would bring them back staggering under the weight of cardboard boxes containing televisions, stereo systems and microwaves. These would be gingerly handed down from the quayside for the perilous journey out to the rusting Soviet ships and eventual delivery behind the Iron Curtain.

The Cold War was full on but there were no passport checks in Ullapool. How many Soviet agents stepped ashore disguised as mackerel fishermen is a figure probably still buried in Moscow files. It was, after all, only another bus ride to the US nuclear base at Holy Loch. It all added to the excitement. The Highlands were awash with cash. The pubs were packed late into every night. Ceilidhs in village halls became wild riots of music and strange accents. You could meet anyone from anywhere. And behind and above it all, when you needed to get away, there was the peace and solitude of the hills themselves. There were always wild brownies in the high, wind-ruffled lochs, ready to hurl themselves at a fly tripped over the waves.

* the 'six o'clock swill' was a NZ phenomenon resulting from a law that forbade pubs to sell alcohol after 6pm. With a thirsty workforce generally finishing at 5pm the name was given to the hour of frantic drinking that followed.

LET'S GO DOWN
TO THE RIVER

SUNWAC: an acronym perhaps recognised by anyone who was at school in the 1950s, before the geography of the British Isles slipped into a backwater of the curriculum. A time when a grasp on the practical workings of the country at the heart of Empire was considered relevant knowledge. A time when there *were* practical workings: ships from the Tyne; leather from the pastures of Leicestershire; coal from the mines of Yorkshire; steel from the foundries of Birmingham; cotton from the Lancashire mills. Before everything came from China. **S**wale, **U**re, **N**idd, **W**harfe, **A**ire, **C**alder: the rivers draining York-shire eastward to the Ouse and the Humber estuary.

On a storm-blown night sixteen years after I first learnt it, that acronym came floating back into my head from the black water swirling at my feet. To the left, five miles down-stream, the floodlit towers of York minster loomed from the darkness. Far to the right, unseen, the distant line of the Pen-nines rose above the Yorkshire plain. In front of me flowed the Ouse carrying water that had fallen as rain on fells as distant as Arkengarthdale on the Cumbrian border. Behind me, a few yards from the riverbank, stood the isolated farmhouse I had just rented for £2 a week.

"Yon place be fairbit damp" the farmer had said, "wall-paper be on floor soon as sun gas in."

Damp was the least of it. When the rain on the fells had

been heavy the centre of York would flood, backing the river over the 'ings' of the flood plain upstream. Then my house would stand isolated on its small hump of higher ground, a ship on an inland sea punctuated by the tops of gateposts and the branches of willows. On clear, frosty nights the moonlit stillness would ring with the whistlings of wild duck. On rare, windless days of blue sky and sun, the water sparkled bright and dazzling. But on blustery days the scouring winds pleated the surface a sullen grey.

In March Tara Tree asked if she could come to stay. Tara had not been born 'Tree' but had changed her name on reaching the age of eighteen. She had wanted something arboreal. Twiggy was already taken*. Branch, Stick, Trunk or Bush didn't really cut it. 'Leaf' might have worked but Tara went for the alliteration. Willow would have better suited her tall, wispy frame better. Flame-haired and fragile she lived opposite Harrods and worked as a model. Her father was very big in flour.

Of course I said yes, and then worried. This was the early '70s, the era of 'the Good Life', of John Seymour and self-sufficiency, of Mother Earth alternatives. I was under the influence of David, my bee-keeping ex-flatmate, and my readings of the naturalist school. With all the fervour of youth I had adopted the ascetic principles of the simple life as promoted by Thoreau in *Walden*. The new house had given me a head start. Original wiring not long post-Edison, a primitive cess pit (not far from the well), no heating or furniture, and a derelict garden. I was cheating on Thoreau a bit – I had a job with the Forestry Commission, a sports car (a hangover from Hoorah Henry days at Cirencester), a fishing rod and a gun. The job provided the funds to buy the four essential foodstuffs I felt it reasonable to omit from a regime of self-sufficiency: cheese, butter, coffee and wine. Rod and gun furnished meat and fish, and the car, apart from normal use, was occasionally useful in providing road-kill if more sporting methods failed. The reclaimed vegetable garden provided the rest.

I wasn't sure if this would be a suitable arrangement for

Tara's two-week stay. Hard times always came in March- the traditional 'hungry gap' when winter crops have finished, spring ones have yet to begin, the shooting seasons are over and it's too cold for fishing. I called her in Knightsbridge to explain the ethics of my life by the river, in other words that there wouldn't be much to eat except cauliflower. That was all there was in the garden. As we were all living out our phase of idealistic youth I shouldn't have been surprised at her reaction.

"I love cauliflower!" she enthused. "Oh how brilliant! Simplicity! Space! Oh, I can't wait! Wonderful!"
She went on in this mode, assuring me my lifestyle was exactly what she needed as an antidote to the superficial life of a London model. I remained apprehensive.

On the second Saturday of her visit she collapsed on the riverbank. She had forgotten the glucose tablets that had been supplying an essential top-up to the cauliflower. With a combination of piggyback and slow hobbling we made it the mile or so back to the house. I must have looked like an ant struggling to haul a stick insect back to its nest. I was not without panic. Were her long periods of sitting silently cross-legged not meditation, as I had thought, but incipient comas brought on by malnutrition? I didn't want any trouble with Mr Hovis. I caved in. In any event, no matter how creative or fanatical you might be in the kitchen, there is only so much you can do with a cauliflower, and we had done it all. Leaving Tara lying on the bed I drove into York and bought a large bag of frozen whitebait and an extra supply of Bulgarian red (it came in 2-litre bottles at a bargain price).

We ate at my newly acquired dining suite, a redundant Forestry Commission map table designed to accommodate large-scale planting maps of northern England. Even though I had sawn two feet off its width, two long-limbed people sitting opposite each other could only just touch fingertips if they half rose from their chairs. This was not a good idea because the chairs were matching banks of old spring-loaded cinema seats in a dusty claret velour. They had been salvaged from a derelict army camp theatre in the forest and the presumably military grade springs would flip them back to the vertical the moment a person began to rise. Children would be sandwiched helplessly. An unwary diner stretching for mid-table butter would drop heavily back to the seat only to find it missing. People occasionally disappeared under the table cursing.

Tara was telling me she had just visited her boyfriend in gaol. This revelation was the most effective barrier to any romantic advance from me that she could have possibly deployed. Not that he was in for GBH or murder or anything violent at all, just a minor drugs bust, but still. She spoke of mean-faced screws in a visiting room heavy with anger and repressed violence. But you couldn't help sensing it was pretty cool to have a boyfriend banged up, at least if you lived in Knightsbridge, though this was long before Pete Doherty and Kate Moss.

That's when my friend Charles burst in, all *bonhomie* and ebullience. Charles had fled the anger and repressed violence of his family farm in the Fens. He has always loved women, can't resist them, flatters them and cherishes them. Little did he realise that on this occasion he would be as a lamb to the slaughter. I went to the kitchen to fry him some whitebait as he folded down a seat. I put the plate in front of him, all white pinhead eyes and tiny tails. Tara was still going on about her boyfriend, presumably fending off any risk of attack from a new quarter. She was intense, explaining that his real problem was not drugs but manic depression. "Manic what?" we asked- it was not a term commonly heard in 1974.

"You know, severe mood swings. Joyous one day, suicidal the next."

The crunching of crispy corpses slowed as Charles listened to the continuing description of the condition. He was realising it mirrored the behaviour of his own father who had enthusiastically bought a new combine and sold it the following week at a huge loss.

"And they've discovered it's genetic-his father killed himself" said Tara.

This morose news quietened Charles who went home early not at all himself.

In the morning Tara let the dog out. It wasn't her fault. Although she knew it was David's old dog she was not to know of the *laissez-faire* principles on which it had been reared, i.e. that it had been left to fend for itself, living off the country as best it could. I had made a start on civilising it, changing its name from the all too descriptive Hoodlum to a calmer Noodle (also appropriate as inevitably it was thin). I was feeding it regular meals, but a door opening onto wide acres of opportunity and a fresh sunlit morning was too much of a reminder of its old life. It was gone.

I guessed she would have headed upstream. This was because I had acquired a kayak that I often paddled up the river to the fast water at Linton weir. A kayak not being designed for passengers, Noodle would follow along the bank, flushing moorhens and hurling herself into the water in pursuit of their skittering retreats. She would sometimes swim the full thirty or forty yards to the other bank to continue the hunt on that side before repeating the process back again. This was a problem at weekends when the banks of the Ouse filled with coachloads of anglers from Leeds competing to hoist the greatest weight of small fish from the river. These fishermen spaced themselves at regular ten metre intervals, each surrounded by the paraphernalia of their trade. Tins of maggots, sacks of groundbait, boxes of floats, thermos flasks and Tupperware full of sandwiches. Noodle saw these obstacles as a fun add-on to the moorhen hunt, leaping over fishing rods like a hurdler getting into stride, with the bonus every few yards of a sandwich snatched from an open lunchbox. None of this ever went down well. Sticks, stones and abuse were often hurled in our direction despite our legal right of navigation.

I walked along the bank trailed by Tara calling 'Noodle-Noodle' into the wind but it was useless. I imagined the dog heading for the watershed on the Cumbrian border *en route* back to Scotland. Anyway I had to go to work. I returned in the late afternoon to find the dog still missing and Tara comatose on her bed, physically and mentally exhausted by several hours of seeking spiritual guidance as to its whereabouts. Unfortunately none had been forthcoming so I set off in the car to hunt the country around Linton.

Passing the village garage I spotted a pair of overalled legs sticking out from under a Cortina on the forecourt. I pulled up, got out and squatted on the oily concrete beside the legs. I inclined my head to shout 'Excuse me' into the space under the car. Like a well-oiled draw a man shot out out on a mechanic's dolly. He remained on his back, spanner in hand, his oil smeared face looking at me sideways rather like a wounded soldier being attended by a medic.

"Sorry to stop you" I said, standing up "but you wouldn't by any chance have seen a black dog loose anywhere?"

"Aye, ah have," he said, "is it yourn?"

"I think it will be" I replied, surprised and relieved at this unexpected response. The man struggled from the dolly onto his feet.

"'s a wild'un is that" he said.

"Aye I know" I said, trying to get into the Yorkshire a bit.

"Lad brought 't in here this marnin'. Ee walks the river Yaark to Boroughbridge every week to see his mother lak. Upset ee was, said dog 'ad set coos runnin', dug oot water rats 'n swum after water hens. Caused chaos lak."

"Sounds like mine" I said.

"Said ee tried to cop it wi' his stick but that kept fol-lowin'. Ah put t' thing in yon loosebox. Poor fella's a bit simple lak. Comes past every week. Right upset ee was."

Feeling relieved at this easy recovery of the dog I said I had bet-ter take it home.

"Yer'll not that," said the man "bludy thing joomped sta-able door. Moost be good faf foot. If yer find yon ah should put 't in steeplechase at Wetherby."

I asked him if he knew where I might find the lad.

"Naah then . . . ah think ee works at livestock maart in

Yark."
I was there at six the next morning.

Beyond the hissing brakes of reversing livestock lorries and drivers hosing out the muck and straw left by their loads I found a thin man in a brown drover's coat splattered with cowshit. He was pushing bullocks along a race with an electric prod. Over the clatter of hooves and the bawling of the bullocks I explained my mission as he kept prodding.

"Yer'll be wantin' Dickie" he shouted "in next shed wit' pigs. Yer'll haft' bear wi' 'im a bit mind."

"Are you Dickie?" I yelled across a pen of jostling pigs to a man, also in a brown coat, this one spattered with yellow paint. He grunted and dipped his head.

"Did you walk up the river to Boroughbridge yesterday?" A repeat of the first signal.

"Did you find a black dog?" At this he started to become agitated. In one hand he held a marking iron with which he was applying blobs of thick yellow paint to the rear ends of the pigs. In the other he held the paint pot into which he periodically dipped the marking iron. Now, attempting to recount his traumatic experience with the dog, he started gesturing with both arms but without putting down iron or paint. Globs of viscous yellow began to fly everywhere branding non-target animals in adjacent pens. Their shrieking was doing nothing to help our understanding of each other.

Trying to dodge the paint and calm Dickie I reiterated what I knew. He had taken the dog to the garage and the proprietor had shut it up. Yes. Then what?

"Ranaway! Ranaway!" Dickie shouted, spluttering with feeling.

"Yes, I know" I shouted back, "but did you see it again?"

" Yes, yes" he said, it had come back to him further up the

river.

Dickie was accompanying his words with a violent nodding up and down of his head and now had his arms out horizontally, flapping them up and down like a bird. Luckily the paint pot was already empty.

"Ranaway, ranaway!" he was shouting again.

Suddenly I got it. Runway! The runway at RAF Linton-on-Ouse. What about it? He had left the dog there he said, at a house at the end of the runway. Realising this was as much information as I could expect in the circumstances I thanked Dickie profusely and left him trying to make sense of the many yellow pigs that were still screaming their lungs out.

By 8 o'clock I had found the farmhouse at the end of the runway but Noodle was not there. The lady who opened the door was apologetic.

"It seemed such a lovely dog but the chap that brought it was very upset it was following him. He said he had to get to Boroughbridge and back to York before dark."

"Did the dog go after him?"

"No. We shut it up to let him get away and then my husband took it to the police station."

"Which one?"

"York. I do hope they haven't destroyed it."

This possibility hadn't previously occurred to me and released a sudden jolt of fear. I drove back to York. The police directed me to their official dog pound.

"Three days," the warden said, "three days we allow 'em. You're in time." Noodle was curled up asleep in a dog-sized cell. It would not be the last time she would find herself detained by the authorities.

*Twiggy- a celebrity model and actress of the 1960s

A DAY OUT

B asically it was a simple land-swop. The Forestry Commission would give up certain areas of the land it held on long lease in return for the estate's agreement that other parts be afforested. Two friendly neighbours might have agreed it in five minutes over a pint. Unfriendly neighbours might argue for years and in this case they had been at it for about twenty. Half a dozen files bulging with yellowing copies of hostile correspondence bore witness. My boss at the Commission handed them to me with the suggestion I might like to engineer a resolution.

The problem had begun with a settlement of death duties following the demise of the old duke in 1949. In lieu of some tax the Forestry Commission had been granted a 999 lease over three thousand acres of moorland for the rent of one peppercorn per annum. The current duke, not unreasonably, viewed this as a very unfavourable arrangement and opposed all plans for afforestation. The Commission on the other hand saw no reason why it should not continue planting those parts of the three thousand acres that it had not already covered with spruce and pine.

The duke had recruited powerful allies in the Ministry of Agriculture, the Nature Conservancy Council and the Campaign to Protect Rural England. He had also chivvied the local authority to align itself against further afforestation, not too difficult at a time when the public was becoming increasingly opposed to large-scale upland planting. The situation was complicated by the presence of a famous beauty spot in the middle of the leased area.

Yet after reading the correspondence and visiting the site the solution seemed straightforward enough. Some parts of our lease provided a reasonable quality of grazing or else were heather moor valuable for grouse shooting. Other parts, the majority, were wet or rocky. It seemed clear we should give up the former, plant the latter and leave the whole two hundred acres of the beauty spot untouched. A sensitive landscaping plan with broad-leaf margins would mitigate the plantation boundaries and improve the grazing areas by providing shelter. It took some time and wads of correspondence but eventually it seemed as if all parties might be able to agree. It was at this point that the Commission's Chief Land Agent descended from headquarters in Edinburgh to see what we were up to. My immediate boss was absent on sick leave so it fell to me to take the chief out to the leased area and explain the various aspects of the proposal.

We met outside the Commission's York office at nine o'clock on a Monday morning. I had been briefly introduced to the Chief Land Agent the previous year at a conference in the Lake District. Ex-army, he was only a year from retirement and had a reputation for no-nonsense severity. The Forestry Commission had accommodated a goodly share of ex-officers after the war and they usually fell into one of two camps. Some saw a post-war civil service career as an extension of military duty, to be conducted with efficiency and discipline, while others treated it as a sort of relaxed semi-retirement after the life and death business of killing Germans. I knew from office gossip that my companion for the day had been in tanks and would undoubtedly fall into the first category.

We agreed to take his car, a large Volvo estate. I put my dog in the back and we set off north on the A19. As he drove I recited the salient points of the proposed deal, the Chief Land Agent occasionally asking for clarification of something. I hoped my ideas sounded convincing, leaving only our imminent inspection of the ground and his approval to conclude a long overdue settlement. My impression was that despite the harsh reputation he seemed receptive and affable so, as we still had an hour of driving in front of us, I ventured to ask about his wartime experience.

"Tanks" he said "flame-throwers."

"Gosh, I didn't know we had such things. Where were you?"

"Normandy to Belsen. Crocodiles."

"Crocodiles?"

"That was what they were called. Fearsome beasts."

I felt a little awed to be in the company of someone with first hand experience of such horrors. The Normandy beaches, flame-throwers, Belsen! Worrying about trees and sheep suddenly seemed small beer. There was a minute or two of silence before he spoke again.

"Top secret, couldn't allow one to be captured. Nor ourselves. Executed on the spot."

"What, by the Germans?"

"They loathed us. With good reason."

Through the next few minutes I learnt that the Crocodiles towed an armoured bowser of jellied petroleum fed to a gun by compressed gas. On approaching a pillbox or other fortified position a demonstration shot would normally persuade the occupants to surrender. If they were bent on heroics an unignited stream of jelly would be fired to saturate the position through cracks and air vents. A third shot would be ignited, setting all alight and incinerating the occupants. There would be no survivors.

My companion was warming to his memoirs telling me of a close call when he had advanced his tank too far and become trapped in a wood encircled by Germans. Attempting to withdraw they had bogged down, managing a fighting escape only after jettisoning the bowser. A reprimand had followed for leaving the bowser in the hands of the enemy. I began to see why some ex-army men could not take peacetime employment too seriously. The chief had fallen silent and as we were almost at our objective I thought I would leave Belsen for the return trip.

My plan for our arrival at this remote block of forest was to attempt the navigation of the forest roads to the highest point of the leased area- a craggy outcrop from where I could point out the lie of the land. We could then drop down to walk about for a closer look. It was late January in a wet winter and as soon as we reached the first clear-fell area it was obvious that any thought of driving to the top was overly optimistic. Heavy harvesting machinery had severely chewed up the access routes. I suggested we get out and walk but I had momentarily forgotten the Chief Land Agent had been in tanks, which was perhaps why he had bought a Volvo cross-country four-wheel-drive model. He had great confidence in it. We ploughed on, slewing from side to side in the mud until finally forced to stop by a large pile of debris. We let the dog out of the back and put on our coats and boots.

It was at this point that I was hit by my first pang of panic. On getting in the car back in York I had noticed my superior's coat lying across the top of a wicker lunch basket, which was covered with a linen napkin. Foolishly I had deemed the heavy coat sufficient protection but I now noticed the napkin was ruffled and no longer spread neatly over the basket. I held my tongue while I tried desperately to think of the best way out of the coming disaster.

Meanwhile we strode off briskly to the vantage point I had in mind. It afforded a good view of the problem areas and the proposed solutions, as I knew it would, having stood there twice previously. We then negotiated our way down the steep hillside to walk some of the area we would forego planting in order to secure the estate's acquiescence to our planting of the remaining, less favourable areas. By the time we got back to the Volvo we had covered a couple of miles of rough terrain and were more than ready for our lunch. As I had feared the Chief Land Agent had not got any, other than a very bruised looking banana. Even a torn packet of crisps was empty.

I admonished my dog (needless to say the ex-David miscreant), which looked briefly sheepish but which I knew to be unrepentant. I apologised in a grovelling way to the chief. I marvelled aloud at how the dog had managed to consume the contents of the basket without alerting us, especially considering the crinkly crisp packet. I could only think I had been too absorbed in the tank stories to notice, while the chief of course had no reason to suspect he had a thief in the back of his car. An admirably surreptitious thief I couldn't help thinking, although of course I didn't say so.

I willingly offered to share the humble lunch I had brought in the pocket of my Barbour coat- a devilled pheasant leg deboned and sandwiched between two very chunky pieces of homemade bread. Unfortunately after pushing through some young plantations the wrapping had suffered and the sandwich now looked a bit gritty with a surface dressing of spruce needles. On catching a sight of it the Chief Land Agent understandably demurred and, as I didn't feel able to eat it in front of him, I made an embarrassed insistence that I buy us lunch at the nearest pub. This was probably twenty minutes away by road once we got out of the forest.

A real problem now arose in that we couldn't get out of the forest. In turning the Volvo around the chief reversed it into a deep hole. The four-wheel drive managed to get a grip but pushed the vehicle forward over a long pole of spruce that jammed itself over the top of the exhaust as far back as the rear axle. We were stuck fast miles from anywhere with no easy way to summon help (this was a long time before mobile phones). The final solution was provided by the two of us lying on our backs underneath the car to take hold of the end of the spruce pole. Eventually, by building into a to-and-fro rhythm of concerted effort, we managed to splinter it into two short enough pieces to be wrenched out from under the chassis. This was not achieved without dislodging the rear section of exhaust pipe from its mounting. Nor without the two us becoming well blackened with peat, mud, wet needles and grease. On regaining hard ground and forward motion I stupidly remarked that at least there had not been Germans shooting at us. This received nothing other than a stony look from the Chief Land Agent who I sensed now regretted having revealed so much personal history to the imbecilic owner of an undisciplined dog.

Our exit from the forest was achieved in the absence of any conversation. This was not so much due to tension arising from the absence of lunch as it was to the difficulty of being heard over the roar of the Volvo's flapping exhaust. I yelled at the chief offering directions to the pub but he shouted back that it was much too late for lunch and we should return straight to York. After a more or less speechless journey (with no mention of Belsen) he dropped the dog and myself back at my car with what could only have been relief. After a perfunctory dismissal he drove noisily off. I sensed the day had not been a complete success.

I was proven right. When in due course my formal report with its recommendations was submitted to headquarters it came back marked 'Unapproved'. It was accompanied by the Chief Land Agent's comment that the Commission was beholden 'in the national interest to take full advantage of our leasehold tenures without reference to any sentiment of freeholders where such might be contradictory to the Commission's long-term goals.' For all I know they are still arguing about it.

ON THE MOORS

After several minutes my boss looked up from the four-page A4 document I had handed him and said,

"What about the forest huts?"

"What about them?"

"Have you valued them?"

"Valued? You mean the little tin shelters they used when they were planting?"

"Some are tin, a few are sectional timber. They all need to be valued."

His tone verged on the patronising and betrayed the civil servant's blinkered acceptance of instructions from above. For some abstruse political reason the Whitehall mandarins had decided it was necessary to revalue the capital assets of the entire Forestry Commission. This only five years after the previous revaluation. Perhaps a question in the House was anticipated.

As land agent for the Yorkshire-Durham area it had fallen to me to put a figure on all our non-forest property such as farms, houses, and recreational facilities. I failed to see the point; it seemed an entirely unproductive exercise but typical of irksome civil service bureaucracy. It had taken me almost a month to do my bit and the summary of my calculations was the document my boss, the land agent for the whole of northeast England, had in front of him. The forest huts he referred to were the makeshift shelters the planting gangs had used thirty, forty and even fifty years previously. Most would have rotted away or vanished into the depths of Sitka spruce plantations. I had given them no consideration.

"Well, we can guestimate how many there might be left standing and put a fiver on each one" I suggested.

"That won't do at all. You'll have to check with the D.O.s and view them" retorted my boss. The D.O.s were the district officers in charge of individual forest areas.

This was the last straw for me. I had been with the Commission nearly six years and although it was a great job I was tired of sitting- either at a desk or behind the wheel of a car. I wanted to do something more physically productive. I was almost thirty and beginning to realise time, unlike the bureaucracy, was not limitless.

I asked the various D.O.s about the huts. Their usual response was a laugh or at least a grin. They confirmed what I had expected, the huts had either been cannibalised for other uses, had collapsed and rotted or were so deep in plantations as to be inaccessible. I reverted to Plan 'A': guessing a number, multiplying by five and fudging the figure into my report. It satisfied my boss but not me. I decided my time was up and informed him it was my intention to resign.

The Commission did not like to lose trained young land agents and there were attempts to dissuade me. The head of all operations for the North-East England region assured me the promotion route to the top of the land agency ladder was clear; 'wide-open' he said, pointing out that all the Commission's senior land agents were at or near retirement age. I reminded him of my recent failure with the Chief Land Agent, thinking that there lay a certain veto of any promotion.

"Pfff..." said the boss man "he'll be gone and forgotten in a month or two. "And," he went on "never mind the salary, think of the kudos!"

At thirty, restless and unmarried, I didn't really care about either. My mind was made up.

As a result the Commission found someone to take my

place. To my astonishment this turned out to be a minor aristocrat, an Old Etonian called Ashton who had been at Cirencester at the same time I had. I think he was entitled to call himself The Honourable George Ashton. Most Cirencester graduates of this ilk fought shy of minor civil service appointments, preferring the big private firms or residential positions on large estates. This was why the land agency field in the Forestry Commission was so 'wide-open'. I was asked to take time to show Ashton around the district before I left.

Most of my work was on the North York Moors, an upland plateau of heather moorland dissected by picturesque valleys, the bulk of the area falling within a national park. In the 1970s the great tide of agricultural progress that was sweeping away traditional family farms or else, in a few cases, converting them into efficient mega-businesses, had by-passed this corner of eastern England. On the moors the Forestry Commission remained landlord to quite a number of tenanted farms and smallholdings. These we had inherited when large landed estates had passed to the government after the war, either in lieu of death duties or following military occupation, or both.

The farming was nothing if not traditional, having more in common with upland Wales than with the arable plains found elsewhere in the east. Most holdings had a few acres of 'in-bye' valley land with grazing rights out on the moor. The steadings were small and old-fashioned, usually an unmodernised stone cottage set beside a small range of cramped barns. Ageing bachelor sons were no rarity, a youth spent in constant work having led to social awkwardness and an absence of marriage opportunities. All owned a tractor but sometimes no car.

One, Eddie Theakston had an old cab-less Fordson Major as his primary transport. Occasionally on winter's days high on the moors I would find him flying along a single track road in top gear, probably heading for some stock sale down in Pickering. His flat cap would be pulled down tight against the snow flurries, his torn army surplus overcoat tied with baler string and only the hill subsidy on a handful of sheep and cattle saving him from destitution.

My job was to keep the rents under review, agree and organise repairs and amalgamate holdings into larger, more viable units when opportunities arose. Consequently I was both friend and enemy to our tenants though I did my best to stay in the former category. I pointed out to my boss in York that for a government agency to be raising rents on primitive properties with no mains electricity, bathroom or indoor sanitation would not look good should the press ever decide to run the story. Thereafter we tried to persuade tenants of the most basic properties to allow them to be modernised. This could be a fruitless exercise.

"Yis, but if yer do up yon place I 'spect yer'll be askin' more rent."

"Well yes, we'd have to, a bit. But we can subsidise that to just 2% of the cost. An increase of maybe £20 a year. Wouldn't that be worth it?"

In the mid-1970s the cost of installing a simple bathroom would have averaged around £1000 and normal interest rates were around 10%. But often the annual rent for the whole farm was linked to ancient low levels and might be no more than £100, and in one or two cases half that. The usual answer was,

"That did well enough fer Father, and Grandfather. That'll do fer me!"

One of our tenants kept geese on a smallholding surrounded by forest high on the moors behind Scarborough. I asked him if I might order a bird for Christmas. A week or so later I drove up to collect it on a darkening December afternoon. His holding was a difficult place to get to, requiring a long negotiation of forest roads before arriving at a field gate. The gate marked the limit of car access, at least in winter, because the final two hundred yards or so crossed a boggy grass field passable only by tractor or on foot. The small stone steading was one of those without electricity or mains water. The water supply was diverted from a nearby beck, running clear and cold through an open trough just outside the kitchen door. In it, dipping and diving, two white ducks were making the most of the demise of the geese that had monopolised this area of the farmyard until a day or two previously. No one was in evidence so I tapped on the door.

The tenant bid me enter a room lit by only one small window that admitted a mere smudge of grey light. I could see nothing at first, although I sensed a presence. Gradually, as in a developing photograph, two lines of pale pink ovals materialised. One, along the end wall of the room, became a long row of dressed geese lying on a trestle table with their unplucked necks and heads dangling floorward. The other line was a row of human faces belonging to several people sitting in silence against the wall in front of me. The tenant introduced me to each as I formally shook hands with one after the other. Six were his adult children and with each introduction he proudly recited their various occupations and achievements. All had left the moors to find well-paid careers in different parts of the country. The youngest was still at university in Leeds, but all had returned to help with the Christmas geese. Rural isolation and medieval plumbing had proved no hindrance at all to their progress.

Being their landlord's representative I was often treated with undeserved deference by tenants for no better reason than that I was in a position to grant or deny their requests. Yet this of course was Yorkshire, famed for blunt, no-nonsense talking which fact tended to keep discussions healthily frank and to the point. Nonetheless negotiations often took place over refreshments that would not be offered to, say, a feed salesman. If I made appointments to visit three farms in a day I knew I would start with coffee and fresh-baked scones at the first, move on to a roast lunch at the second and finish with tea and cakes at the third.

Outside the tenant and I would walk wind-blasted fields or stare up into the rain at leaking barn roofs. Inside we would strip off wet coats and boots and settle ourselves around a table in the warm fug of a small, cluttered room. Usually a damp collie would have slipped between our legs to fall onto a rag rug beside an open-fired range. It would be gently booted aside by the tenant's wife who, clutching protective tea towels, would bend to the oven before proudly rising with a hot tray of proper warming Yorkshire fare. On such days brimming mugs of weak, milky coffee came thick and fast, occasionally leavened by warming shots of stronger stuff. It was the latter that cursed me with an unwanted reputation during my first winter in the job.

The tenant of one of our larger farms had invited me for a day's pheasant shooting in January. As civil servants we were instructed to be cautious about such things in case they could be construed as 'backhanders'. I justified my acceptance by seeing it as a useful and traditional way of getting to meet some more members of the local farming community. Knowing how cold it could be standing about waiting for driven pheasants on top of the moors I filled a hip flask with malt whisky before leaving home. This flask had been given to me as a present at some point and had some serious design defects. Most significantly it was made of glass encased in leather so that rather than becoming nicely dented with use, as would a traditional metal flask, it could be broken or cracked. Secondly it was far too big, holding about half a pint instead of just an ounce or two. This one, unknown to me, had a hairline crack concealed by the leather wrapping. I slipped it into the pocket in the lining of my Barbour coat.

At lunchtime I was abashed to see the rest of the shooting party retire to a barn with their sandwiches while the tenant invited me alone to join him in the farmhouse for a hot dinner. The outside temperature was at or just below freezing. This had prevented the whisky molecules from escaping the lining of my coat, which they had been gently permeating all morning. But now, in the sudden heady warmth of the farmhouse, they seized their chance to fill kitchen and lobby with the fermented barley atmosphere of a Spey-side distillery. I think it was Macallan. The fumes were intense and quite inescapable, catching everyone by surprise, not least me. I saw the tenant look at his wife who was busy about the oven. I'm sure I saw him roll his eyes meaningfully. Seeking to mitigate this embarrassment with an explanation I withdrew the flask from my coat. The dark saturation of the leather confirmed the source of the problem but pushed up the alcohol content of the room even higher.

"Ah" I exclaimed in a voice trying to emphasize both sobriety and innocence "this bloody flask is leaking!"
But I don't think it did any good in averting an instant reputation as a drinker because once we had finished eating the tenant was quick to produce a bottle of his own malt and suggest a dram. He must have been convinced he was holding the key to his landlord's good favours. On re-joining the rest of the party back in the yard I felt sure I was moving inside an aura of volatile whisky fumes detectable by everyone. I did notice that during the afternoon they all took care to stay out of range of their host's guest.

This was the work environment with which I had to acquaint Ashton during my last weeks with the Commission in the spring of 1977. We took several trips around the moors together as I showed him various projects and introduced him to our tenants. As I have said most of these were straight talking, blunt Yorkshiremen farming small, unviable and un-modernised holdings, places barely able to provide a living. I was apprehensive that Ashton's rather plum-in-mouth autocratic style might not go down so well in this marginal upland community but I was quickly shown to be mistaken.

We had just visited the tenant of a particularly rough and boggy fifty acre farm on the moors above Pickering. It was a filthy day of horizontal sleet and I was looking forward to gaining the lunchtime sanctuary of a pub in Thornton-le-Dale. As Ashton and I stood in the muddy yard saying our goodbyes to the tenant I remarked on a small, sick looking Angus cow standing hunched under the shelter of a lean-to.

"That doesn't look too good" I said nodding in the direction of the cow.

"Nah," said the tenant "got leg stook in manger an' twisted her back lak. Vet said can't do owt forrit."
Ashton perked up.

"Perhaps I can help," he said.
I looked at him wondering what on earth he had in mind.

"Doot yer will" opined the tenant.

"Get me a coat of some sort will you?" said Ashton.
The tenant went back into the house and came out with an old donkey jacket that Ashton put on backwards in the manner of a surgeon's gown. I thought he might be getting ready for some mad Etonian style prank. He approached the cow that in its misery made no attempt to move away. Leaning over it he felt carefully along its nobbly spine then stood back a fraction, steadied himself and gave the animal's back a sort of karate chop with his right arm. It looked ridiculous but the cow did give a sort of small jerk before settling back into its previous pathetic pose. The tenant and I both stood slack-jawed watching this procedure as Ashton walked back removing the coat. He handed it back to the tenant saying in his best BBC voice,

"That may possibly help. I think it's quite badly hurt. You'll see in a day or two."
I thought he was being absurd but the following week I happened to pass the tenant repairing a roadside fence, so I stopped to pass the time of day.

"Nah then" he said.

"How's that cow?" I asked, expecting it to hear it had been carted off to the knackers yard.

"New fella's some lad in't he?"

"How do you mean?" I said.

"Little black coo's good as gold. Runnin' about like a

heifer. If yon man can do that sort o' thing he'll be right lad to have hereaboots!"

I drove on feeling more than a little chastened. I was right in one respect though. The Commission was not the job for Ashton. He left after a few months to become a chiropractor to thorough-bred racehorses.

CORNER FARM

T he Kielder dam in Northumberland sits on top of my friend Chris's farm. Literally. It was only a small upland farm of fifty acres or so with a cottage that Chris's family used for holidays. The land was let to a farming neighbour. But both house and land were compulsorily purchased in the early 1970s as the site for the dam that would flood the upper valley of the North Tyne to create Kielder Water. Before the dam Chris used to fish for trout in the river. There were no salmon because they couldn't get through the toxic sludge choking the river at Newcastle. Now, in the post-industrial age, the river is full of them and Chris's stretch would be worth a fortune, if it wasn't under the dam. The relative upside of the compulsory purchase was that the money allowed Chris to buy a smallholding on the Yorkshire Wolds not far from the village where his father was a vicar.

Corner Farm was not big enough to provide a living without some sort of intensive enterprise being introduced so Chris went into a working partnership with his school friend Philip and set about developing a pig breeding business. Both of them were in their mid-twenties and refugees from the careers they had been trained for. They set to with enthusiasm, each day's work underpinned by the steady excitement of building their own business after a period of restlessness. Progress was slow because there was very little money left over after the purchase, which meant that everything had to be done on a shoe-string, but Philip was a practical sort of person with an aptitude for construction and Chris was a hard worker. Both were also outgoing, sociable types and so found their farming neighbours ready with help and advice.

The house that went with the farm was small and cramped, built largely of lumps of chalk chiselled from the surrounding wold. Chalk, of course, is porous, making such constructions permanently damp and cold, but Corner Farm was unusually cold for two additional reasons, one immutably geographic, the other voluntary. The geographic was that at an elevation of six hundred feet above the coldest coast in England the house was exposed to freezing northeast winds sweeping in unbroken from northern Russia and the Arctic Ocean. The voluntary freeze factor was that Chris and Philip saw expenditure on anything other than the pigs as frivolous and possibly unnecessary. So, in an effort to leave as much money as possible for investment in the farm, basics such as heat and food were reduced to the minimum necessary to sustain life. In their first winter they considered it great good fortune that their neighbour had grown a field of swedes for his sheep just over their boundary hedge. Road-kill supplemented by mashed swede was Corner Farm's standard *plat du jour*. This ascetic life-style in pursuit of a goal became a forceful philosophy in itself, bringing an atavistic delight in the return to hunter-gatherer mode in an age of plenty. The fun came whenever there was an opportunity to shock those whose domestic lives were more conformist.

Being sociable sorts, a large measure of the excitement the two found in their new endeavour came from discovering the various characters and personalities in the community around them. They knew there were two locations that, apart from business connections, would facilitate their integration into the village: church and pub. Both boys came from church-going families, with Chris's father a vicar and Philip's about to become one, so attendance at services in the church opposite the farm gate came naturally. Nor did it cost anything other than a few pence in exchange for a snippet of wine and a wafer. The pub required readiness for a heavier financial input, however generous their fellow drinkers might be, but Philip and

Chris decided a Friday night pint or two at The Butcher's Arms was not only a good investment socially but a well-earned reward for a week's work. Unlike Corner Farm it was also cosy and warm with an open fire kept burning all day for nine months of the year.

One activity in danger of being omitted from this routine of work, church and pub was romance or, more bluntly, sex. A small farming community on top of the Wolds held only limited opportunities for two single young men. There was the Young Farmers' Club but Chris and Philip were getting a little too old for that, and in any event they felt that working all week with pigs was more than enough agriculture. Wider horizons were needed.

The East Riding of Yorkshire is a very rural area and The Butcher's Arms, not being a poshed up gastro-pub, tended to host the same clientele from week to week. Nonetheless on Friday nights Philip and Chris kept their eyes open for any 'talent', or even anyone who could be justifiably described as 'young' as the average demographic of the village was close to or above retirement age. So when two women in their twenties appeared one week, albeit escorted by two males, they were quickly engaged in conversation. The women revealed they were teachers sharing a house in not-too-distant Pocklington. By the end of the evening both had been invited to dinner at Corner Farm the following night, although this had necessitated inviting the unwanted boyfriends as well. Dinner parties were not a usual feature of life at Corner Farm and after issuing the invitation and having it accepted the inviters did not give it much further thought, particularly as any logistical thinking was blurred by the intake of several more pints.

Saturday was a working day with the pigs and it was not until about 6pm that the arrangements made for that evening came into focus by reason of their imminence.

"What shall we give them?" Chris asked Philip.

"Anything in the freezer?" said Philip.

"Only those plums from the churchyard."

"You could drive over to your mother's and see if she's got anything."

"It's twenty miles, they'll be here in an hour."

"I'll take the van for rabbits."

"See if you can get a pheasant by the wood."

Philip came back half an hour later with two run-over rabbits, one found in reasonable condition and one freshly bagged. These were subjected to the standard Corner Farm recipe:

- Skin and gut
- Throw in roasting tin
- Place at top of electric oven,
- Turn temperature knob to max.
- Do not forget to add whole unpeeled potatoes.

As Philip was dealing with this cuisine a tap on the door indicated the four guests had arrived. Both hosts were horrified and momentarily embarrassed to see the boys had dressed themselves in jackets and ties while the girls were wearing dresses. It seemed the visitors, having received an invitation to dinner from Wolds farmers, had assumed the affair would be a semi-formal one indicative of the affluence generally seen as attached to that profession. They must have been surprised to find Chris and Philip still in their overalls even if their approach to the house had forewarned them of the smell.

Anyone who has ever had anything to do with farming pigs will know there is a particularly indelible odour associated with the business which percolates through farm, farmhouse and, most especially, clothing. In most cases it is held under control by energetic routines of regular cleaning and laundry but since taking possession Chris and Philip really hadn't had time for that sort of detail. After all, the furniture was only salvage from the local dump. The tatty sofa and various stained easy chairs looked unlikely to let the visitors escape without incurring a subsequent dry-cleaning bill.

Despite their best efforts not to show it the guests were visibly shocked at the reality that had so suddenly replaced their expectations. For Chris and Philip this was all part of the fun, but they were far from cruel so Chris immediately sought to put all at ease with friendly chatter and the offer of a drink. Unfortunately even less thought had gone into the evening's liquid refreshment than into the meal itself. All the house could offer was a bottle of sweet British sherry. Chris had picked this up on a visit to the supermarket after noticing a sign reducing its price to 99p. His eyes now fastened on the bottle of decent red wine one of the boyfriends had placed on the kitchen table. Not one to stand on ceremony he added this to his offer but not before all four guests, anxious to recover their equilibrium, had politely said the sherry first mentioned would be fine thank you. It wasn't of course, but this they were left to discover for themselves as Chris ushered them towards the fire he had lit in the sitting room. The wine would do for the meal.

Philip, realising that an additional supply of alcohol might be necessary to ensure the success of the evening, excused himself by saying he was just popping up to the Arms' to collect some beer for the boys and would be back in a minute. A minute was of course an optimistic assessment of the time it would take to enter a Saturday night pub full of merrily drinking friends and acquaintances, buy some take-away beer and return home. Despite the urgency it was well over half an hour before Philip returned to find that Chris, left single-handed to entertain all four guests, had not thought to check on the cooking. Consequently the kitchen was full of pungent smoke, the oven still being on maximum heat. Philip opened the outside door, flushed out as much of the smoke as he could and called the diners through.

Once they had been seated with beer and wine before them, and the ice at least partially broken, he opened the oven door. The room and its occupants were immediately enveloped in rolling billows of greasy black smoke. Breathing became difficult. As the guests coughed and waved their hands up and down in front of their faces Philip, his hands protected by a sacrificial tea towel, bent to reach into the oven. He grasped the almost molten roasting tin and quickly hurled it onto the bare wooden surface of a kitchen table that bore the scars of many previous brandings.

It there was to be going to be a moment when the guests would up and run this was it. The two blackened corpses, entire and unjointed, looked not so much like rabbits as two napalm victims from some unedited newsreel of the Vietnam war. Their empty eye sockets seemed fixed on the onlookers and tufts of burnt fur still decorated the feet. Philip in his haste had skinned them whole leaving the carcases untrimmed. He now bent again to the oven with the smouldering tea towel and threw out a salvo of steaming, flaking potatoes that crumped onto the table like so many dummy mortar rounds. He then stood surveying his handiwork. A paralysis seemed to have gripped the guests.

"Don't hold back, help yourselves!" he exclaimed.
Sensing the meal might seem intimidating to those unaccustomed to subsistence living, he grasped one of the corpses in his bare hands and dismembered it, throwing various ripped-apart sections onto the plates of those seated. Mercifully, owing to the excessive oven temperature, only the meatiest joints still showed traces of blood under their blackened crust. The dinner was completed with bowels of the stewed churchyard plums, un-stoned, unencumbered by cream or custard and notably lacking sufficient sugar.

To their credit the guests took no offence at this trial by burnt rabbit and reciprocated with an invitation to supper in Pocklington the following month. This second evening inevitably followed a more conventional format than the first but, more importantly, the continuing presence of the two boyfriends made it clear that these were long-term fixtures, unlikely to be dumped. This realisation took the hare from before the hounds and the two farmers returned home accepting they would have to give up this particular chase.

Heterosexual though the boys were it was inevitable that two single men farming together and living in the same house would engender suspicions that things might be otherwise. Their readiness to chat up and flirt with any female they encountered below the age of fifty might have been seen as evidence to the contrary but unfortunately the opportunities for even this activity were curtailed when Chris unwittingly fell foul of the local young mothers

Shortly before the Christmas of their first year Philip took a weekend off to travel south in search of female companionship. Chris, left to look after the farm, was soaking in the bath after a smelly day with the pigs when he heard the sound of carol singers in the yard. This was just a tad irritating because in order to get enough hot water for a bath either the open fire had to be kept going all day to heat the back boiler, and/or the immersion heater had to be switched on. The two scrimping business partners considered any of this an extravagance and so inevitably shared the water, tossing a coin to see who would go first. The loser would often abandon his turn on seeing too great a depth of surface scum. Chris had therefore taken advantage of Philip's absence to enjoy the luxury of a bath taken without arousing objection or the risk of being second. And now here were carol singers interrupting his pleasurable soak.

Not that Chris objected to carol singers. Quite the reverse, he has always appreciated the traditional aspects of country life and, hot water apart, his heart warmed to the sound of 'Good King Wenceslas' floating up through the freezing December air.

The problem was that the lights in the kitchen and upstairs clearly signalled that someone was at home. If he simply laid back and enjoyed being serenaded in the bath the carollers would leave unacknowledged, undoubtedly assuming the new residents at Corner Farm were miserable skinflints. Chris was certainly not miserable, nor did he want these community minded people to think that he was. He abandoned the bath, girded his loins with a towel and hurried downstairs to the kitchen door. He threw it wide open and announced in his most welcoming voice,

"Would you all like to come into the warm?"

The previously energetic singing of 'The Holly and the Ivy' whimpered to a stop. There was a moment of complete silence, quickly followed by subdued female giggles. The boys just stared and grinned before the adults, with outstretched arms, shepherded their youthful flock away towards the road. The reason for this sudden curtailment was that the stout and sturdy Chris in his haste to support community activity had snatched a mere hand towel to cover himself. This was nowhere near adequate for the job. The incident set back his social integration by several months until the rumour branding him a perverted exhibitionist was eventually accepted as unfounded.

Despite this hiccup all came well in the end. Chris married Sarah, a local farmer's daughter, and Philip married Liz, the sister of a friend. He moved into a cottage just up the road from Corner Farm and housekeeping budgets in both homes became marital arrangements rather than business principles.

POTLUCK

B ruce, my old school friend from Arizona, bought forty acres from the Oregon Forest Service. It had been cut over once for the first-growth Douglas fir but the re-growth was big enough to provide him with logs for a simple cabin. To build a log cabin you have to fell the trees in May when the sap is rising so they can be barked cleanly and easily. Then you cut rough tongues and grooves along their length so the walls will keep out the wind and rain. This is all done with hand tools. It's a slow and laborious business.

Bruce had a job as night watchman at the lumber mill on the river so building the cabin was taking longer than it might have done if he hadn't had to sleep for many of the daylight hours. The upside of the job was that he could take home discarded off-cuts of milled timber for things like windows and doors. While he was building his house Bruce lived in a teepee in a meadow beside the creek that ran through his land. When I visited him there in the 1970s he was one of many young refugees from California hanging out in the woods. Woods that hosted many small clearings growing marijuana. Most nights there would be a gathering at somebody's place. People would bring potluck dishes of food and packs of beer. We would sit around a campfire talking and drinking but if Bruce was working he would have to leave early for the mill.

I stayed for a month during which Bruce or I never once washed up. In the evening we would immerse the day's dishes and pans at the edge of the creek. By the morning swarms of crayfish would have picked off every vestige of food or grease and everything would be as clean as a whistle. Every now and again Bruce would put a wire trap in the creek and we would pull it out full of these miniature lobsters clambering over each other clacking their pincers. We boiled them in a pot over the fire and ate their delicious tails with mayonnaise, lemon and black pepper. It seemed fair enough.

FRANK CATCHPOLE

It's well known that forced exposure to a ceaseless drip or repetitive noise is an effective torture. Combined with, or as the cause of sleep deprivation it can drive a person mad. I knew I was going in that direction as the relentless tap-tap-tap continued through sleepless post-midnight hours. Intermittently an interlude of blessed stillness would deliver the hope that ninety-year-old Frank next door had at last fallen asleep in his chair. Or with his two sticks had levered himself across the kitchen to his bed. Or died. Sometimes, masochistically, knowing it would only increase the pain, I timed these silent intervals in my head. Twenty, twenty-one . . . hope would begin to strengthen . . . twenty-four, twenty-five . . . continuing silence, hope rising further. Twenty-six, twenty-seven . . . thank God, he's stopped. Twenty-eight . . . oh God no! The tap-tap-tap would begin again signalling that Frank had positioned the next apple log on his hearth and little by little was reducing it to shards of kindling under the repetitive strokes of an antique billhook. Despairing of sleep I would pull the pillow over my head with a sideways squint at a bedside clock that crawled through the dead hours toward dawn and work back up at the farm.

Not that Frank was in any way trying to be un-neighbourly: it was simply that his internal clock was beholden neither to any external one nor to the natural rhythm of sunrise and sunset. Throughout the day sleep stalked his brittle frame where he sat in a hardback chair beside a concrete hearth and ancient stove. Periodically he succumbed to its stealthy advances that usurped any plan he might have had to actually *go* to bed. And when, with a shiver and shake, Frank re-awoke, at whatever hour, he would bend forward over the hearth to continue his eternal task of splitting the apple logs the foreman brought down from the grubbed orchards of the farm. *Tap-tap-tap*. Obsessively splitting them into ever-thinner sticks to be fed into the firebox of the stove. Keeping his small withered body warm and alive with a purpose. *Tap-tap-tap*. Three in the afternoon or three in the morning, summer or winter, it was all the same to Frank.

His few needs were arranged on a table within arms' reach. A loaf of sliced white bread, seedless jam (small seeds were a menace to his dentures), margarine, a packet of Bakewell tarts and another of processed ham. Replenishment was taken care of by Mrs Bloomfield when on Mondays, Wednesdays and Fridays she came in to do the necessaries. Propped in the corner on Frank's other side was a four-ten shotgun, an old fold-in-half poacher's model with skeleton stock and a single barrel speckled with rust. Next to it stood a paper sack of wheat into which Frank would sporadically delve a wooden scoop, flicking the corn past the open back door to his few ageing hens. These had no hesitation in crossing the threshold to follow the trail of spilt grain to Frank's slippered feet. Beneath the table a chamber pot served for those occasions when Frank's dicky legs were not up to the struggle to reach the privy outside. The fowls occasionally eyed the contents curiously but had the sense not to explore further.

The gun was for the rats that thrived secretively but with great fecundity in the wilderness of once-garden that crowded up against Frank's back door, a brambley jungle pierced only by a short tunnel of trodden-earth leading to the brick outhouse. The rats' success was partly due to the largesse of corn and food scraps which they boldly appropriated from under the beaks of the chickens. This brazen theft annoyed Frank who, on spotting a rodent through the open door, would let fly with the four-ten from where he sat by the stove. Unfortunately the coordination of the old poacher's rheumy eyes and unsteady hands were not as once they had been. The usual result was that, as the rat scuttled off into the undergrowth unhurt, the shot would rake through the unsuspecting chickens, one or more of which would be left twitching on the path, mortally wounded. Cursing, Frank would struggle to the fatality and hurl it away into the bushes. As the chickens decreased so the rats increased, a sort of win-win situation from their point of view.

It was when it became necessary to talk to Frank for some reason or other that the path to his door became seriously dangerous. On these occasions I would squeeze through a gap in the bushes behind the outhouse before flattening myself against its rear wall and, with head turned sideways, extend a waving hand into the space above the path while shouting

'Frank, it's me! Don't shoot!' like some gunslinger in a bad Western. Actually stepping out onto the path was always an anxious moment.

Although Frank callously discarded the martyred hens as too old and tough to bother with, his night-time roamings of earlier years had left him with a great fondness for roast pheasants. Late in the year these would be attracted to their favoured roosting sites in the tangled thorn bushes behind Frank's half of the cottage. The cocks always foolishly announced their presence by crowing loudly as they fluttered up in the dusk. This usually proved too much for Frank who would hobble down the path on only one stick, his other arm crooked around the fourten. Propping himself against the trunk of a dead apple tree or the outhouse wall he would raise the gun toward the silhouetted bird, quietly cock the hammer and pull the trigger. Sometimes the pheasant would fall dead through the branches but just as often Frank would overbalance into the brambles. As the season wore on it became touch and go as to who was at greatest risk of death, man or bird, until eventually the procedure became that Frank would summon me with a double knock on our dividing wall. In his kitchen he would thrust the loaded gun at me with something like:

"There's a cock-bird gone up at the far end of the hedge

boy. Just go and get it for me."

By January there were never many left.

Frank plucked these pheasants sitting in his chair by the stove. The upward draught of heat would waft the downy under-feathers into a gentle grey snowstorm that settled over the room, sizzling on the hotplate of the stove, sticking to the margarine tub and the plates in the sink and coating the bed with a thin, random eiderdown. Most of the feathers proper Frank shoved into the firebox of the stove which would then begin to produce a smell like the back end of a crematorium. The guts were thrown out through the door to be recycled by the chickens and rats, and the carcase itself went into the oven on its way to sustaining Frank for more *tap-tapping*.

One November day in 1979 I ran the gauntlet of the path to let Frank know that early in the new year I would be moving to another tied cottage a few miles away in Heveningham. He averted his eyes.

"Huh! Yew on't like it."

"Why not, what's the matter with Heveningham" I retorted defensively, "you said you spent half your working life in Peasenhall just down the road from there?!"

"They're a bloody rum lot. You'll see," said Frank with the assumed authority of experience, signalling the end of the exchange.

A day or two later Mrs Bloomfield was getting ready to leave on her shiny new moped as, on my old push-bike, I arrived back at the cottage for lunch.

"I hear you're leaving us," she said inquisitively.

"Afraid so" I replied, "I've sorted out a better arrangement on a farm in Heveningham. Mind you, Frank seems to think it'll be worse."

"Yes, well, that will be because of poor old Florrie," said Mrs B.

"His daughter?"

"She married a pigman in Heveningham who turned out a right bad sort, knocked her about, so they said."

"Oh dear, he never told me about that."

"He wouldn't. Anyhow then he ran off with the neighbour's wife in the middle of the night. Old man Wright had to feed the pigs himself until he found a new man and when he did he chucked Florrie out of the house without so much as a by your leave. She lived with Frank and his wife for years before she got a council flat in Ipswich. Far as Frank's concerned anyone in Heveningham is tarred with the same brush."

Florence was Frank's only child, a thin, chest-less woman in her late sixties who had neither had children with the errant pigman nor remarried after his sudden leaving. On her rare visits to her father she usually wore a tired grey flannel skirt below a drooping button-front cardigan, the pockets stuffed with tissues with which she constantly dabbed her nose. She bore the look of a woman for whom life had passed slowly with scant pleasures. As she didn't drive her visits were dependent on the good nature of a female acquaintance from the Methodists who brought her out from Ipswich. In truth there was little other than filial duty to attract her, for when she did arrive the squalor of Frank's cottage upset her tidy mind, eventually provoking her to inquire at the council offices as to whether he might be moved into a home. We exchanged telephone numbers against the event of any urgent need to contact one another in relation to Frank.

One lunchtime in early December a small red car was parked on the road outside Frank's half of the cottage. As visitors were a rarity I walked around to the kitchen door to check that Frank was not being scammed into buying new windows or an exotic timeshare. A pert young woman with short black hair and an air of efficiency stood with a clipboard ticking boxes on a form. I could see it was headed *Assessment for Residential Care: Critical Score Sheet*.

Having identified me as the immediate neighbour she

asked me one or two questions concerning Frank and continued ticking. I could see headings such as *Cooking Facilities*, *Personal Hygiene Arrangements* and *Mobility*. A large space had been allocated for *Officer Comments* and here at the end of a lengthy paragraph of neat handwriting I noticed our interrogator had written 'Some sort of gun is present and appears unsecured'. From this sentence an arrow guided the reader's eye to the margin where she had added in smaller writing- *refer to relevant authority*. This she must have done for on the Wednesday of the following week a police car was parked where hers had been, its presence a little unnerving as my mind raced over my own possible failures in licences, tyres, road tax, dogs or guns.

As soon as I entered my half of the cottage Frank's double knock summoned me to his kitchen where a large policeman in a black vest decorated with a two-way radio and silver numbers explained that as Mr Catchpole had no shotgun certificate he should by rights confiscate his shotgun then and there. That was the law. But it required a deal of paperwork and Mr Catchpole had proposed that perhaps I could take charge of the weapon forthwith and take it into Richardsons' gunsmiths in Halesworth to see if I could at least obtain a few pounds to compensate for its loss.

In his chair Frank was jiggling one of his sticks up and down between his knees, a sure sign of agitation, for the policeman had tactlessly pointed out that the gun might as well go as it certainly wouldn't be allowed in the nursing home. Talk of any imminent move to a nursing home was news to Frank. Though he did remember Mrs B. had said something about her rota possibly being re-arranged. Bureaucracy was closing in on Frank with a sense of inevitability. I promised to take the gun into Richardsons' the following Saturday afternoon after work.

Two days later, pruning up in the orchards, it did not seem particularly unusual to hear the siren of an emergency vehicle approach the village and then stop. People were always having heart attacks or strokes. I did not anticipate finding an ambulance and a police car blocking the road beside the cottage. The ambulance had its rear doors open, its lights still silently flashing. In the back I could see Mrs B. sitting on a bench seat: a blanket was over her shoulders, her hands to her face. A paramedic was kneeling in front of her proffering a mug of tea. The same policeman was sitting in the passenger seat of his car, his legs out through the open door, talking into his radio. Looking up at me he broke off:

"You were supposed to take that bloody gun off him! What happened? There'll be all hell to pay now. Don't go in there. Forensic's on the way from Martlesham."

I felt dizzy and sick. I noticed the concrete pathway to Frank's was stained with dark footprints.

Whether there was hell to pay for the policeman I never found out. For my part attendance at the inquest was officially the end of the matter. The verdict was 'accidental death'. Mrs B. was positive the coroner had got it right, she was surprised it hadn't happened long ago: the gun was always loaded, the hammer loose, Frank doddery. And the shot had been to the neck, not in the mouth or head. Florrie too was happy with the verdict. Afterwards I sometimes worried that I should have taken the gun away, but then I don't think Frank would have let me. He didn't see it coming to that.

PEARL

The obvious problem with living in a 'tied' cottage on a farm is that a decision to quit the job to do something else also means finding somewhere else to live. If you are just married without any money this can be awkward.

'Young married man seeks part-time agricultural/forestry/horticultural work in return for accommodation'

I thought that wording, placed in the classifieds of the East Anglian Daily Times, might do the trick. It promised the energy of youth coupled to the responsibility of a married man with no need for actual money to be paid out. Meanwhile as I had promised my employer I would vacate her cottage by the first of January 1980, I thought it prudent to arrange a fallback position. Under 'Property to Let' I found a holiday cottage in Laxfield available on a winter let until Easter at the appealing rent of only £10 per week. Over the phone I agreed to put down a week's rent to hold it. It would be a stopgap but it would keep a roof over our heads. Maggie and I thought we better have a look at it in case nothing else turned up.

At some time the cottage must have been convenient. At least for the occupant's work, assuming that was in the surrounding fields. Located at the end of a long, unmade track it failed on every other convenience, being miles from the village and unconnected to mains electricity. There was a diesel generator that powered a pump in the well, pushing water up to a tank in the roof, but if you wanted that water hot it was necessary to keep the open fire burning fiercely all day to activate the back boiler behind it. This open fire was also the only source of heat as the generator was too small to handle any electric appliances other than basic lighting and the water pump. Not even an electric kettle. Instead a scarred blackened thing of ancient manufacture spent its life in the fire or on the small propane camping stove that served for cooking. Holidaymakers might have loved this 'back to basics' but probably not as much as getting home again. There was a rudimentary bathroom but no inside loo, this facility being about thirty yards distant from the back door in the traditional brick outhouse. In the early '80s when winters in Suffolk brought long spells of snow and ice our December viewing did nothing to encourage the prospect of a cosy marital home. We just had to hope the phone would ring with alternative offers. It did, several times.

Beyond the gate lodge the drive deteriorated badly. By the time it had crossed the remnant of overgrown parkland and entered the woods it was clear from the size and depth of the potholes that this was a track for four-wheel-drive vehicles only. Fortunately we were in one, my old ex-army Land Rover. The trees closed in overhead, the undergrowth squeezed in from both sides and just as we thought 'this can't be right' the low timber-framed hall appeared in front of us like a giant's lair in a fairy story. No vehicles were in evidence, nor any other sign of habitation. The pressing greenery had lightly brushed the whole of the rambling building with a moss coloured patina. Weeds and seedling trees had mounted an attack on the roof, sprouting from gutters and hidden roof valleys. At ground level brambles and feral roses had been roughly hacked away from their siege of the gothic-shaped front door. Bound in heavy iron and pitted with age the latter was clearly a medieval original. A tug on the rusty bell-pull beside it set off a noisy jangling inside but nobody came. After a decent wait I pulled again with no better result. I tried twice more and was about to leave in search of another entrance when I caught the sound of shuffling steps followed by the double 'clunks' of bolts being shot open. The door swung slowly inward to reveal a stooped, elderly man in dowdy slippers and a brown tweed suit worn over a mustard pullover.

"Ah" he said "yes, the young man. And his wife presumably. Come in."

He beckoned us in with one hand before turning to shuffle off across the tiled floor of the hall towards a doorway. It seemed we were to follow. Our single file procession of three entered a large room completely panelled in dark oak, including the ceiling. It felt as if we had walked into the giant's coffin. There, facing us in an armchair beside a log fire, sat a second man, physically and sartorially identical to the first.

"This is my brother Andrew. I'm Toby," said the man we had followed in. Clearly the two were twins close to eighty years old. Andrew raised his eyes to look at us and slightly dipped his head but made no attempt to stand. Neither man had offered a handshake. I sensed they lived here alone together in arboreal isolation.

"Bring over a seat," said Toby indicating some hardwood chairs at a table as he himself dropped into a threadbare armchair on the opposite side of the fire to Andrew. I carried over the chairs and Maggie and I sat stiffly between the two men. They both regarded us without speaking for several moments as we stared at the burning logs. I wondered if I should say something. It felt rather strange.

"Do you have children?" asked Andrew suddenly.

"No" I said "we've only been married since August."

"Will you have any?" he said.

This was something Maggie and I had not yet discussed in any great depth. We looked at each other. She frowned discreetly at the intrusion and I said

"Well yes, hopefully, in due course."

"Dangerous place for children, the woods" said Andrew.

"And they do make such a lot of noise" added Toby.

"Well, that's not a problem for the time being" I countered, "Exactly what sort of work do you need someone for?"

"Pruning, high pruning" answered Andrew.

"High pruning?"

"Yes. Oak and ash mainly. Can't grow a quality butt, not unless it's been properly encouraged you know."

In fact I did know as the result of the forestry lectures at college. But the high pruning of hardwood forest trees was an archaic practice that had died once wages exceeded half a crown a week and half the country's labour force had perished in the Great War. I was also certain that these two living Victorians would have no modern high-lift equipment but would expect the pruning to be carried out from the top of a ladder, work that would be practically synonymous with suicide. Yet I had to admire the selfless intentions of these aged men, given that the pruned oak would deliver no return on the investment for at least another half a century.

"How many days work each week would you expect in return for the lodge cottage?" I asked, having been told on the telephone this would be the accommodation offered.

"Well I don't know," said Andrew "I take it you would want to go off somewhere else?

"Yes, that's the idea. I'm trying to get my own nursery business going."

"Yes but there are three hundred acres of woodland here you know. A lot of it needs pruning. And then there's the firewood."

"And the rats" added Toby.

"Rats?"

"And the damn squirrels," continued Andrew " you just need to remember to put poison down once a week, and tend the traps. Oh, and a bit of gardening now and then and the odd building repair, nothing much, a little painting. Do you know anything about plumbing?"

There must have been a shortage of people willing to climb ladders with chainsaws that year because our next interviewer wanted someone to spend two days each week cutting high level branches from poplar trees. This made slightly more sense than doing it to oak but not much because the market for poplar was collapsing fast with the expiry of the Bryant and May match empire. Then there was the apple farm with five hundred acres of apples to prune. Having just quit a monotonous pruning job on a small apple farm with only twenty acres I couldn't face it. Next came a call from a member of one of Suffolk's most aristocratic families who said he needed a gardener in exchange for a flat in the hall.

An appointment was made for 5.30pm on a Saturday. At the time I was keen on shooting and Maggie and I had spent the day on a shoot near Ipswich. We arrived at the hall wet and muddy, in a Land Rover, with two Labradors and a heap of pheasants in the back. "Well," I said as we scrunched up the gravel of the drive "at least they'll think we speak the language." Our potential landlord-cum-employer must have seen us coming as he stood waiting for us at the open main door. He greeted us with enthusiastic handshakes.

"I'll show you the flat," he said, leading us through into a kitchen where a bevy of laughing, posh-sounding females took very little notice of us as they chopped and stirred the food for a dinner party. We were led on into a dining room where a long table was spectacularly set with crystal, linen, silver candelabra and flamboyant flowers. An open staircase ascended along one wall of this room. We followed our leader up these stairs to a sort of landing-cum-minstrel gallery with a door leading off into a small one-bedroom flat. The flat was nice enough but I immediately saw issues with the logistics.

The owner confirmed there was no access other than via

the kitchen and dining room. It seemed obvious that getting in or out in the middle of a lunch or dinner party might be embarrassing or, at the least, inconvenient. On the up side, if our passage should coincide with episodes of wine-fuelled hospitality it might be entertaining. Certainly it was clear that entertainment and hospitality played a significant part in the life of the house. For his part his lordship seemed much less worried by the potential for the disruption of these social occasions than I was.

"Oh don't give it a thought" he charmingly assured us "most of these dinners would benefit from a bit of interruption!"
Nonetheless it would mean living in intimate proximity to our landlord and his family. We felt our newly married life required a little more independence.

As Christmas approached it seemed inevitable the new year would see us forced into a Spartan life amid the fields of Laxfield. Meanwhile Christmas was to be spent with Maggie's parents in Newcastle. On the morning of Christmas Eve we loaded the Land Rover with our bits and pieces, settled the dogs on top and were preparing to lock the door when the telephone rang. "I've seen your ad in the East Anglian" said a male voice "I farm at Heveningham- Alan Fairs. I need someone to keep the garden tidy and help on the land now and again. There's a decent cottage."

We locked up and drove straight to Heveningham. We looked at the cottage and at the farmer's garden. We discussed the job and the terms.

"Well, give it some thought over the break," said Mr Fairs.

"No need" I replied, "we'll take it. We're happy if you are."
And so we trundled up the A1 towards Christmas in the frozen North, safe with the comforting thought that we would be returning the following week to a house with hot water and an in-

side loo. And new neighbours instead of Frank.

We moved the five miles to No.2 Dairy Cottages on New Year's Day. We took our sparse belongings, including the contents of the freezer, piled in an open trailer converted from an old muck spreader. We lost only one frozen chicken on the way, and that might have been down to the dogs.

No.1 Dairy Cottages was occupied by Don and Pearl. It was the superior dwelling because it was larger and had had central heating installed. Don was head tractor driver on the thousand-acres surrounding us, an arable holding based on the old home farm of Heveningham Hall. Pearl was one of a number of rural ladies who, in the days before the English gave up low-paid jobs, kept local agriculture going by hoeing and trimming sprouts, 'rogueing' cereal crops and picking potatoes, apples and strawberries. I did not come by an introduction until the following day. It was not to be an auspicious start.

The rear garden of No.2 was bounded by a tall and over-grown hedge of mainly ash. Seeing that this blocked the light of the westering sun from the back of the house I took a chainsaw to it as my first job on our first morning in residence. The bigger stuff would make excellent fuel for the kitchen Rayburn but the smaller lop and top I set alight in the middle of the garden. Stupidly I failed to look up enough to register the presence of a telephone cable overhead. Ash, even green ash, burns easily and well and it wasn't long before the insulation on the low hanging cable began to melt and drip into the fire. I was wondering how best to deal with this problem when suddenly Pearl came flying around the corner of our shared outbuilding shrieking

"You've set my house afire!"

I rushed back in her wake to find a large stack of firewood piled beside an oil tank. From within this stack a thin curl of smoke was lazing upward. Really it was a storm in a teacup because once I had pulled the stack apart and doused some smouldering leaves with a bucket of water the fire was out and the panic was over. Nonetheless there had been the potential for something spectacular given that the oil tank was nearly full. Foolishly I then made the prospect of friendly relations even more remote by saying,

"Well it's a good job we don't need to call the fire brigade because I think I've melted the phone line."

In fact I hadn't because a fortunate breeze had developed which prevented the heat of the fire playing directly upon the copper cable, leaving it intact if unprotected. As I recall it stayed that way for the next several years without causing any problems except for a bit of a crackle on the phone if it was raining.

I never saw much of Pearl after that because she always left for work at 7am sharp on her Honda 50 and went to bed as soon as her favourite soap finished at 8pm. I discovered this early bedtime by accident. The front lawn of our semi-detached house had no demarcation between Nos.1 & 2 so whoever was cutting the grass cut the whole lawn. Thinking it must be about my turn I started up the mower at about 8.30 on an evening in early July and was trundling back and forth when the front door of No.1 flew open. This was very surprising because Pearl and Don never used their front door and I had assumed it was inoperative. But there in the open doorway stood Pearl in a startlingly diaphanous nightdress shouting something I couldn't hear over the sound of the mower. I stopped it as Pearl repeated her complaint with restrained fury.

"Some of us have to get up in the morning you know!"

This was not only a complaint about the mower noise but also a sideways slur on my perceived laziness at not leaving home to begin *my* workday until after seven. It was also a confirmation of Pearl's own faultless work ethic.

After about a year without further confrontation Maggie suggested I should ask Pearl if she might be interested in helping to cut the field of asparagus I had almost ready for harvest. At first I shrank from the idea, certain I would receive short shrift at the proposal. The truth was I was a little afraid of Pearl's severe manner and in awe of her ascetic lifestyle. But I plucked up the courage to ask and Pearl consented and so we began a working relationship that lasted over thirty years until shortly before she died. No matter where we moved or where the work was, Pearl would be there ready to start at 7.30 a.m., regardless of a commute of up to twelve miles through winter weather on that same 50cc Honda. This reliable machine was maintained by Don, was never changed over thirty years and was still going when Pearl gave up. Not that she gave up voluntarily.

In the early years we sold much of our produce at the roadside through an honesty box system. Eventually dishonesty made this practice unviable and I adapted a shed into a primitive farm shop supervised by Pearl who filled the time between customers weighing, trimming and packing the fruit and vegetables brought in from the field. Pearl was extremely conscientious, took her work seriously and became expert at presenting the produce with a professional look. Her interpersonal skills were more contentious. Her brusque, no nonsense manner, combined with an old-fashioned shyness of strangers, sometimes gave the impression of rudeness. She could be terse. Customers expecting a flood of friendly chatter in response to a question might be disappointed for Pearl had nothing in common with graduates from the modern 'have a nice day' school of customer relations. She became something of a USP because of it. Especially when she teemed up with old Arnold.

Arnold was married to Nancy and Nancy was someone Pearl approved of heartily. Of similar age the two women had been brought up in neighbouring villages as part of large families and had known lives of hardship and hard work. Both were extremely punctilious. But if Pearl was always on time in the morning she was also unwavering about finishing at 4.30 in the afternoon. This allowed her to get home with sufficient time left in the day to get her chores done, watch the soap and get to bed by 8pm. The problem was that 4.30pm was a little too early to close the farm shop once it had grown into a larger operation. Nancy volunteered Arnold to take over for an hour from 4.30 to 5.30pm.

Arnold was another Suffolk old-timer. He had retired from the local 'river board' and was not a man for wasting words. A customer might ask,

"Have you got any strawberries?"

"No."

The customer might wait for elaboration but none would come.

"Will you have any tomorrow?"

"Don't know."

"Do you think it will be worth my while calling in then?"

"You can please yourself."

At which the customer would leave, appalled at such rudeness. The face of modern retailing this was not, a fact that some of our local Suffolk patrons were rather proud of. Luckily Tripadvisor reviews were in the future.

In due course I found a tenant to take over the running of the shop and that marked the end of the old regime. Pearl was by then too old to return to field work and so retired to her garden in Halesworth. Here Don found her face down on the grass one afternoon, prostrated by a stroke while planting daffodils. She was rushed to hospital where I visited her a day or two later. She was sitting up in a wheelchair in a dayroom. Seeing me enter she struggled to get words out from the side of her mouth not immobilised by the stroke,

"I blame you for this!"

"What do you mean?" I exclaimed, bewildered.

"Overwork!"

There could have been a grain of truth in that.

STARRY STARRY NIGHT

It's nearly midnight but the night is still T-shirt warm, even here on the beach. No moon, but great swathes of stars reflecting off a mirror-flat sea. Crescents of sudsy foam sweeping the sand smooth in front of me. And going round and round in my head an unseasonal verse:

'Star of wonder, star of light, star of royal beauty bright, westward leading, still proceeding, lead us to thy perfect light'.

A Christmas carol in mid-August? Madness! But why not?

'We three kings of Orient are, bringing gifts we travel afar, moor and mountain, field and fountain, following yonder star.'

Word perfect.

We showed that fucking consultant and his fucking forceps! He didn't like that, no he did not. Some peasant like me questioning his authority in front of his nursing staff. But we did it. No forceps, no cutting, no painkillers. Good old Sally midwife, she knows her stuff. Incredible really, nearly everybody's done this amazing birth thing and then they get over it and everyone's so calm, so ordinary, as if nothing much ever happened in their lives. And now I'm a capital 'd' Dad. Forever. How amazing is that?

'Walking back to happiness, oompah oh yeah yeah. Say goodbye to loneliness, oompah oh yeah yeah.'

Helen Shapiro, 1961. This is getting like Desert Island Discs. Talking of walking and dads I'm heading along the beach to The Dolphin to meet mine.

Oh shit ... I don't want this, not now. It's like watching TV with the sound off. I can see them through the window- a table full of noisy people, drunk or heading that way. I knew it would be like this. I really don't want to go in, don't want to risk losing the elation. But what the hell, it's fading anyway.

I go in. An explosion of pushed back chairs.

"Hey, here's the man!"

Firm, meaningful handshakes. Strong eye contact. Slow-motion embraces into perfumed cashmere breasts. But Dad's eyes as he staggers up from his place at the head of the table- swimming, glazed. Empty. For God's sake Dad.

So I tell them: no intervention, no drugs, no forceps, just coconut oil. Sandy says "Coconut oil?" so I say:

" You just massage it in and the skin stretches."

"Who rubs it in?" asks the arsehole Ron.

Now Dad plays the absolute idiot with inappropriate comments, at least as far as I'm concerned. Jesus wept. I go upstairs to phone the news to the in-laws on holiday in Cornwall. It's blowing an absolute hooly down there. I can hear the wind over the phone.

"It's a bit wild here," says the campsite lady "but Jim will go with the message now."

I hear her tell him to put his oilies on. Doors are banging. She says some empty caravans have gone over the cliff. Thank God for other people.

Now Dad's going on about Valerie eating his untouched grilled sole.

"Why won't you eat my sole? You don't love me. I give you my sole."

She's had enough of being embarrassed in front of her friends and ignores him. I have to leave. As I do he says he's proud of me. I wish I could reciprocate. Oh I really do. Outside it comes on again:

'Bringing gifts we travel afar, moor and mountain, field and fountain following yonder star'.

Maybe it leads to Ipswich Hospital. Or wherever you want it to. There's the Orford light, a single flash every five seconds. A warning.

HENRY

Our first crop of asparagus at Rattla Corner got us started. In the early '80s the crop was beginning to make the transition from a luxury for the well heeled to a commodity vegetable sold by the supermarkets. Plantings were on the increase and an English growers' association was formed for the exchange of information and the general promotion of asparagus eating. That it was still a minor crop was evidenced by the discovery that with only six acres I was the second largest grower amongst the membership. Most of the crop I sold to a local company that packed for the supermarkets but we also sold a good deal 'at the gate' of the bungalow in Knodishall we had inherited from my mother in 1984.

Knodishall is a sprawling village of mainly modern, single-storey housing, its landscape badly disfigured in the 1960s by huge pylons carrying the transmission lines from the Sizewell nuclear power station. It lies about five miles northwest of the affluent coastal town of Aldeburgh. Aldeburgh is an altogether different kettle of fish with pleasing aesthetics and a decidedly more middle and upper class population. Including, until his death in 1976, the town's most famous son, Benjamin Britten.

Just outside Aldeburgh, on the main access road into the town, Henry Baldry farmed at Grange Farm as a tenant of the Blackheath estate. Henry's farmhouse, set on rising ground to the north of the Alde valley, had a marvellous view from its south-facing windows over the marshes and the estuary to the North Sea. Huge white ferries passing in and out of Harwich on the Hook of Holland route moved slowly across a horizon that looked to be on the same level as the farmhouse.

The problem was that for most of the summer Henry couldn't see them because the field in front of his windows was light and sandy which meant that in most years it was cropped with rye. Rye grows particularly tall quite early in the season and obscured the view. Henry's wife thought this a great shame. So did Henry, who was no slouch on aesthetics having worked in fashion design in London before returning to the family farming operation. Henry thought about it and decided the answer was asparagus. Asparagus demands sandy soil and is kept cut at ground level until well into the summer. It is also a long-lived perennial crop that, Henry reasoned, would provide a year-to-year answer to the view problem. He also suspected that Aldeburgh, only a mile away past the golf course, would provide a ready market. Henry's first asparagus crop came to harvest a year or two before mine and was an immediate success.

In fact Saatchi and Saatchi could not have designed a better blueprint for Henry's operation. For a start everyone going into Aldeburgh went past it. And then went past it again on the way out as there is only the one main road in and out of the town. The town's resident population included a high proportion of asparagus eaters and was swelled at the height of the asparagus season each spring by many more of the same attending Britten's by now world-famous Aldeburgh Festival.

As for the detail of 'the retail format' it was better than perfect. Once you had turned into Henry's long daffodil-lined drive you progressed upwards between two fields of growing asparagus. The view of field workers stooping to its harvest would add to the authenticity of the experience. As you continued a picturesque set of traditional ivy-covered brick and tile farm buildings appeared settling into a pleasing state of disrepair. Wild rabbits would be popping to and fro across the track. You skirted around the old buildings and continued uphill to a large modern barn surrounded by acres of grassy space on which to park. On entering through the open doors of the barn you were greeted by subdued classical music and huge, comfortably worn Persian carpets that led you to an improvised counter of old potato bins. Behind this a line of local ladies chatted merrily as they trimmed the asparagus into the traditional bunches. As you left you took in the stunning views of sea and estuary.

Then came Henry's masterstroke. Princess Margaret occasionally stayed with Sir Eric and Lady Penn at nearby Sternfield House. Seeing Henry's rough-painted but pleasingly bucolic sign advertising asparagus the princess's party had called in and bought some. Henry promised to send further supplies to Kensington Palace. Finding these well received he followed up by including Buckingham Palace on his annual gift list. The resulting official letters of thanks were framed and prominently displayed beside the sales counter in the barn. *Her Royal Highness wishes to thank . . . etc'*. Of course that went down a storm in Aldeburgh. So much so that the producers of the tremendously popular radio programme *Down Your Way* interviewed Henry in his capacity as purveyor of asparagus to the royal family first and captain of the golf club second. Henry's asparagus was on the national map.

Demand was so great that Henry never had enough. He telephoned me. Had I any to spare? Henry's price was a good deal better than the supermarket's and in any event it was good to do business with a friend and neighbour. So began my nightly runs over to Henry's in a pickup filled with boxes of asparagus. I usually arrived at Grange Farm just before dark between 9 and 10pm. I would drive up to the walk-in chiller in the big barn and stack the boxes inside. Often while I was doing this Henry would show up in jacket and tie having just returned from the bar at the golf club. I would always greet him with

"How are you tonight Henry?"

His answer would always be the same,

"Pissed and penniless!"

He was often the former but never the latter, at least not since he'd begun growing asparagus. He would usually tell me to call at the house on my way out to pick up some cash. There, in the old-fashioned kitchen with its big cream coloured four-oven Aga he would hand me a wad of notes and try to persuade me to stay long enough for a whisky or two. I rarely did as Henry's whiskies were large. Exhausted and unfed as I would be at the end of a long day, even one would have made getting home a perilous and illegal venture.

This arrangement worked well for both of us but gave rise to the situation in which some of our Knodishall customers would swear by our asparagus and vocally condemn Henry's as awful, while several of Henry's customers stated the reverse, not realising it was more than likely the same stuff. But Henry certainly had the marketing edge with his set-up. If I was delivering on a Sunday evening he might confide to me in a whispered aside some astonishing amount he had taken over the weekend. This worried me a little.

"Henry" I said on one such occasion "you know it wouldn't take someone with a lot of brain cells to work out you might have a lot of cash in here at night. You know, a stream of smart cars coming up your drive all day."
Henry and his wife were becoming aged and Grange Farm stood alone amid the fields.

"Ah, I've thought of that" answered Henry, "I've put most of it inside a hollow tree up the lane!"

That did not put my mind at rest as to the old couple's personal safety but a 'tree bank' satisfied Henry's own security concerns. In the event nothing untoward ever occurred during the several years that business continued before Henry's death in 2006, though I've often wondered if he made a full withdrawal of these liquid assets before he died. If not perhaps some squirrel has a nest papered with old ten-pound notes. The irony in Henry's success with asparagus was that in seeking to preserve the view from his front window he had somehow overlooked the cultural necessity of allowing the crop to grow to full height once cutting ceased in late June. The asparagus fern grew a good deal higher than had the rye and completely obliterated the view from July until Christmas.

OVERLOAD

Sally was a midwife who ran antenatal classes in north Suffolk in the 1980's. There was then, and still is, a healthy alternative current in this part of the county and Sally was well supported by expectant parents eager to be encouraged towards natural childbirth. Epidurals, episiotomies and forceps were out: birth pools, coconut oil and soft music were in. All good stuff. If there was a downside it was that Sally's militant opposition to the interventions of mainstream obstetrics tended to engender a 'them and us' attitude: Sally's imminent mothers sometimes entered maternity wards on a war footing. It all worked well for us however and by the time Maggie was carrying our third child we felt we had got it off 'pat' with no qualms about choosing a home birth this time around.

Murphy's Law came into play two days before the due date by causing our cesspit to overflow. This catastrophe rendered all domestic drainage inoperable, including the two WCs that threatened to overtop if flushed. Now in a situation clearly not acceptable for a home birth I hurried over to borrow a friend's mini-digger and set about digging up the driveway. The plan was to lay a 100-metre run of drainage pipe from the offending cesspit to the main sewer at the gateway, a utility to which the property had never been connected. My mother, living frugally on her own, had not seen the point of paying sewerage rates. Now her economy had come back to bite us on the bum.

I soon got the hang of the digger and excavated a deep trench the length of the drive. The tricky part was finding the main sewer pipe at the edge of the track that ran past the gate. This difficulty was not surprising as it was nine feet down which meant operating at the limit of the digger's capability, not to mention mine. It is amazing the amount of spoil that comes out of a hole! Both sides of the drive were lined with low mountains of sandy soil making vehicular access impossible. The immediate impression was of trench warfare. Nevertheless I felt the solution to our problem was in sight.

The next day was the May Day bank holiday which became unusual in that, despite being a bank holiday, a heat wave blew in from the south escalating the temperature into the mid-80s Fahrenheit. Not ideal for blocked drain work but first class for asparagus growth on which the main part of our expanding family's annual income depended. That year, 1990, we had a vigorous new ten-acre plantation coming into its first full season of production. In the heat it took off like a rocket. That's another one of Murphy's laws- asparagus always grows fastest on a bank holiday when it's impossible to find workers at home and you have to pay them double if you do. Nonetheless a few panicky phone calls resulted in a small emergency crew turning out including a lovely, if forceful, young lady called Jackie recently arrived from Glasgow. Jackie persuaded one of her new neighbours to come along to keep her company. Neither of these two ladies had done any field work before so I took some time to explain the importance of only putting into the crates spears of the right length with tight tips, leaving in the field those that had grown too long. The latter were to be cut off but not picked up as they were worthless.

Happy that the situation was vaguely under control I hurried back to the pressing issue of the drains, taking with me the full crates of asparagus already cut. Of course the packing shed and cold store were at the top of the now impassable drive. Fortunately our neighbour's driveway ran parallel to ours on the other side of the hedge. Agreement was swiftly reached for our use of this alternative access, despite it requiring a sizeable hole to be cut in the hedge through which the crates could be passed.

Eventually I got the asparagus into the cold store and returned to the sewer.

The daunting bit was the prospect of breaking into it with the new overflow pipe. Was the main under pressure? I knew it was pumped- would the creation of a hole result in a high-power jet of human waste hitting me in the face? Worse, was it possible the main itself might fracture and flood the whole neighbourhood with shit? Or, if the joining went smoothly, might there just be a slight delay before the mains pressure backed up to the house and filled it with other people's shit. All these imagined scenarios also carried the prospect of angry Anglian Water personnel and stupendous fines, if not incarceration.

I am not a plumbing professional but thank heavens the good men who originally laid the main were. Grubbing about in the sand nine feet down I discovered they had had the foresight to provide an 'eye' in our gateway against the prospect of a future owner desiring a connection. An unusual stroke of foresight on my part was that I had assembled from our local builders' merchant a number of different types of connectors in the hope that one might be the right one for the job. Nevertheless at nine feet down in a narrow trench it was fairly difficult to work out which one it might be and the relentless heat and blue sky demanded I get back to the asparagus before the harvested stuff wilted.

I could have cried.

"Aye but ye said ter cut the jaggy eens 'n leave t'others on the floor." said Jackie, taken aback at my anguish.
Hundred of yards of prime, top-value asparagus lay in wilted rows in the sun while dozens of crates of over-long, worthless 'blown' stuff stood stacked on the headland.

"Didn't the others say anything?" I asked.

"Nae, nae, they're all awa' workin' at the far end. We two just thought we'd do this wee piece here."

"Ah well never mind, too late now but next time it's the other way round."

"OK, but ye didna mak' yersel' clear." said Jackie defensively.

She was probably right in her assessment of my management skills but I did have a lot on my mind. The departing gang agreed on a 7a.m. start for the next morning in an effort to finish before the afternoon heat. I collected up the good asparagus, dumped the Scottish contribution and headed up the neighbour's drive to shove the crates through the hedge towards the cold store. It was soon full to its doors and working on overload. As we all were, including the drains and, not least, Maggie.

Back in the trench I felt things were roughly going to plan although my plan did omit the legally required inspection chambers, rodding eyes and pea shingle bedding normally installed with such works- there just wasn't time for the niceties. One nicety I did wonder about was temporary shuttering. Fudging about on your knees at the bottom of a narrow nine-foot-deep trench in sandy soil with the spoil piled closed to its sides is a significant first step in irreversible self-interment. A coroner would be obliged to decide suicide as opposed to accident. Or terminal stupidity in leaving a new baby fatherless.

A slightly less mortal fear, as the evening wore on, was that one of the homeward bound cars passing on the nearby road might contain Jeff Whitely, our local council's building inspector. Jeff lived in the village and I vaguely knew him on a professional basis. Good sort that he was, he was also the sort cast from the mold that insists on good practice and proper procedure in every situation. That's what building inspectors do, along with keeping their eyes alert for clues to uninspected, illegal developments. Jeff would be completely apoplectic should he catch sight of my project. He would order an immediate stop before probably calling the public health people and perhaps the police. It was not as if the operation could be carried out discreetly- the towering heaps of spoil lining the drive were a dead giveaway.

Consequently I was grateful for the cover of darkness which found me with a torch and a bucket of wet cement crouched over the main sewer pipe. Through the narrow slot above me stars twinkled in a clear sky promising endless blue for the morning. A nightingale was singing in the gorse bushes on the common. A baby was to be born. A brief moment of serendipity occurred but evaporated when a check on the cold store revealed that, faced with the insuperable task of cooling over a ton of asparagus from 20º to 2º, it had let all its refrigerant gas escape through a crack in the pipework. More plumbing, but this time well beyond my capabilities. A desperate late night call to the refrigeration company got through to the duty engineer who promised to have someone with us by 7am.

At 7am the field team was wondering where I was, not because I had been delayed by the refrigeration engineer, but because it was at 7am that Maggie started her labour. There were calls to make. First to Pauline the Welsh midwife with news of the labour and explaining about the neighbour's drive and the hole in the hedge. Then to the asparagus buyers to let them know we would (somehow) be delivering; and then a call to try to catch the asparagus cutting ladies with instructions for the new day. Then it was standing by for action after briefly popping out to brief the refrigeration engineer. To get at the faulty pipe he was faced with emptying the whole store of un-cool asparagus by himself. 'Sorry, I must go- my wife is having a baby' is a guiltless excuse, if a rarely available one.

Through the bedroom window I noticed Pauline's Clio shoot up the neighbour's drive. I hurried out to guide her in. Pauline is a lovely lady but short, with legs to match. Sturdily built, I doubt she would describe herself as athletic. I found her balanced on top of the spoil heap opposite the back door, holding tightly to her large black medical bag.

"I can't get over that!" she wailed, peering down into the depth of the trench.

"Yes you can Pauline. I'll catch you, throw the bag over first".

She gave it an underarm swing and it disappeared into the trench.

"Never mind I'll fish it out it in a minute" I assured her. But the bag mishap had unnerved her. She wobbled; limboed backwards with rotating arms, over-corrected forwards, and began to fall.

"Jump Pauline, Jump!" I encouraged desperately.
She sort of hopped and fell at the same time, collapsing forwards like a tree bridging a stream. I caught her under the armpits and for a moment it looked as if we would both slide to the bottom of the trench bringing it down on top of us. But it was one of those 'mother-lifts-a-bus-off-child' moments and heaving backwards I fell with Pauline on top of me.

"Are you alright?" I enquired in a concerned voice.

"Right as rain," said Pauline struggling to get off me and straightening her tunic "but don't expect this on every visit!"
Fighter pilots call this 'the right stuff'. The doctor arrived and, being athletic, made an impressive entry leap. Being also well acquainted with the principles of alternative birthing he took a seat in the living room and read the paper so as not to be intrusive. Purely back-up.

By the end of the afternoon Lizzie had been born without complication, the asparagus had been cut, the cold store was up and running and I had made a dash into the buyer's depot with the cooled asparagus of the day before. The best bit, after Lizzie, was being able to flush the loos. Once everything had calmed down a bit I set about filling in the trench which made life a lot easier all round.

Over the coming years our improvised drainage system worked a treat despite the lack of 'niceties' but somehow we never quite got round to notifying the authorities of the improvement. As a result we missed out on bills for sewerage. Well, 'sleeping dogs' I say. Mind you, when the house was sold its drainage provision took a bit of explaining. But Lizzie was 22 by then and I was an asparagus baron.

DOUG

In the spring of 1980 I had been cultivating the field at Rattla Corner when a man had pushed through the hedge and stood watching me. Heavy set and dressed agriculturally, he stayed at the edge of the field looking interested so when the tractor drew level with him I stopped it.

"Morning" I said.

"What the hell are yer doin' on?" he replied in a tone which could have signalled either incipient humour or aggression.

"Getting it ready to plant asparagus" I answered.

"That on't work."

This left me undecided as to his intent.

"Why not?"

"This field in't nevva grown nuthin', tha's jist a sandpit."

"Well, I'm gonna give it a go" I said, a little dismayed by the depth of his negativity.

"You want a bigger tractor to pull that," he said continuing in the negative vein. This was true as the little Ferguson tractor I owned was struggling with the cultivator I had borrowed.

"Well yes, but this is the one I've got."

I probably said this last a bit sharply because I was feeling that a word of encouragement would not have been out of place. My new acquaintance made no further comment but turned and left through the hedge the way he had come.

Reflecting on how some people are doomed to see only

hopelessness, I restarted the tractor and continued cultivating. Not many minutes later I heard the chug and clatter of an old tractor passing along Church Lane and spotted the top of its exhaust laying a smoke trail above the hedge. It appeared in the gateway to the field with the cause of my reflection on hopelessness at the wheel. He got down and walked heavily across the field towards me. I stopped my tractor again and waited for him.

"If you bring that over we'll try it on my International" he said, "tha's fifty horsepower, that oughta pull the bugger a bit better." Which it did and he flew up and down the field until the surface was all perfectly fine and level. It took about an hour while I trimmed some overhanging branches out of the way. When he was finished I asked what I owed him.

"Bunch of asparagus" he said straight-faced "but I doubt you'll ever git it orf here."

At the time Doug and his wife June lived in a cottage at Rattla Corner but a year or two later they moved to a new mobile home just across the field from Reckford Farm. In 1994 we became neighbours. Doug had built a large barn for June's pigs and added several lean-tos to keep his cattle in during the winter when they came in from the marshes. June loved her pigs and Doug loved his cows. In the summer Doug made some hay and grew a half-acre of potatoes and June cultivated tomatoes in a polytunnel.

Our three young daughters would toddle over to find June and ask if they could see the baby pigs. After letting them play with the little pink wigglers for a time June would ask each girl if they would prefer a present of a choc-ice or a £1 coin. At first the decision this required caused a huge amount of discussion and consideration because £1 empowered the holder to purchase any number of permutations of 'penny' sweets from beside the till at the village garage, whereas a choc-ice was a choc-ice, pure and simple. Later the girls realised the choice was in any case academic as on their departure June would give them whichever item it was they had rejected, no matter that they had already received the one chosen.

Doug's particular strain of humour persisted. After we had lived at Reckford Farm for about a year he came out with,

"I reckon you've aged ten years in the one you've bin here 'bor."

Or, seeing me planting Christmas trees,

"You must be feelin' hully optimistic today 'bor."

I would return compliments in the same vein. Passing Doug one Monday morning on my way down to the asparagus I stopped to say good morning. He was laying heavy concrete blocks for another extension to the pig barn and complained of pins and needles in his hand.

"Oh, is it your left one?" I asked.

"Yis" he said, shaking it vigorously as if to rid it of the nuisance.

"Well you know what that is," I said, "you're having a heart attack. I expect I'll find you lying here dead when I come back for lunch!"

He flipped a trowel of wet cement at me and I drove away. On the Friday I bumped into his son Colin at Rattla Corner.

"Haven't seen your dad about lately" I said "is he on holiday?"

"Yis" said Colin "in intensive care at Ipswich. Heart attack last Monday."

"Oh my God" I exclaimed and went off to visit him that night to assure him I had meant no harm. 'Many a true word is spoken in jest' was one of my grandmother's favourite aphorisms.

Doug survived that one successfully. He was a big man and had been a tough one, spending most of his working life in the iron foundry at Leiston Works. But at heart he and June were agriculturalists and in their spare time had always kept stock on bits of rented land here and there. Before moving to

Rattla Corner they had lived in one of the pair of farmworkers' cottages set above the road just beyond the bridge at Reckford Run. Here in the garden they kept a large sow called Alice. Every few months they would walk Alice over to Watson's boar at Vale Farm to be served. The difficulty was that the route necessitated passing through a thick hedge atop a ditch. Doug and June could scramble through the gaps but getting Alice through was another story. She always baulked because the tangled thorn and brambles played havoc with her sensitive snout. June struck on the idea of putting a bucket over her head for protection but that only made matters worse because of course like that she couldn't see where she was going and careered off along the bottom of the ditch in a blind panic until the bucket fell off.

The next time Alice was due for service Doug decided they would partly mechanise the operation by transporting her to the Watsons' in the back of their old Morris Traveller, the estate version of the Minor, the one with external woodwork and double doors at the back. Luring Alice into it using an old door as a ramp and a generous trail of pignuts ending just behind the front seats was easy enough. The problem came after they had shut the rear doors and set off along Fen Street towards Vale Farm, a distance of about half a mile.

Alice was unsettled, close to panic again, and the Morris was an old one. The floor of the rear compartment had not been designed for the hooves of a large sow weighing the best part of half a ton . It gave way bringing Alice's rear half in contact with the road while her front portion scrabbled desperately to stay in the vehicle. All three occupants had to continue in this configuration in first gear with Doug slipping the clutch to give Alice's furiously trotting rear trotters a chance to keep up with the rest of her. On reaching Vale Farm she was eventually extricated by using a tractor to hoist up the rear of the Morris while persuading Alice to reverse back through the hole in its floor. It was the next day before she had calmed down enough to stand for the boar. The car was a write-off.

Doug had long suffered from diabetes. It was circulatory

issues arising from this that eventually saw him off at about the time the new millennium began. June asked if she could hold the wake at Reckford Farm. I was unable to be there as I found myself in hospital on that very day. I thought at the time that Doug's dark humour would have approved of that obstacle to my seeing him off.

The cattle had gone but June carried on with the pigs for a time, though her heart had gone out of the job. In remembrance of Doug she planted an oak sapling in the hedge near the mobile home, shortly before she herself was diagnosed with cancer. After she had gone, which did not take long, the local authority began to agitate about the mobile home as it had been permitted under only a temporary agricultural licence. Colin, finding it too difficult to remove, knocked it to bits with a digger and burnt the bits. The pig barn remained, gradually collapsing into dereliction and becoming home to a nesting barn owl and numerous pigeons. I occasionally cleared choking vegetation from around Doug's oak tree. It's now thirty feet tall, a salute to them both.

THE SHORTEST DAY

It was four days before Christmas. Maggie hated the way it had been hijacked by the consumer society as just another sales opportunity. The scrums at the supermarket, the gridlocked traffic, the incessant advertising, the endless lists, the extra work. She knew she couldn't pull it off this time, not in the circumstances.

I was at the kitchen table writing cards. She sat down opposite.

"Jack"

"Hmmm?" I didn't look up from writing but said   "What was Maggie Laine's new partner called?"

"Victor"

"I thought it was Ian."

"That was the previous one."

I wrote Victor into the card.

"Jack"

I looked up and met her eyes.

"I'm having an affair."

For a moment the words floated, disconnected, in the Aga-warmed kitchen air. I suddenly sensed their threat, like noticing a hornet slowly crawling up your arm.

"Say that again."

"I'm having an affair."

"You're joking. Mags, that's not funny."

"I'm not joking."

"With who?"

"I can't say."

"Since when?"

"The early summer."

"I don't believe you, you are joking."

My mind was racing, catching up with hints I had been too stupid to see. I got up and went over to stand by the sink. I thought I might be sick.

"With who?"

"I can't say."

"Maggie you have to say-I might be sending him a fucking Christmas card for Christ's sake!"

"He's not on the list."

"Mags, this is not right, you have to say-please."

"Bob"

"Bob? Bob the builder? You can't be serious!"

"Yes Bob the builder, Bob the brickie. He loves me."

This seemed unlikely, no, impossible. She was always at tennis lunch parties with friends. Bringing home news of holidays in Sardinia or safaris in South Africa or pools and tennis courts being installed by merchant banker husbands. Bob was a pudgy little guy from Essex who lived in a council house with Doreen and two grown up children.

"This is ridiculous. You can't love him"

"I think I do."

"For fuck's sake!"

I was walking around the table, head in my hands, muttering.

"Jesus Christ, Jesus, Jesus."

This wasn't going the way Maggie had hoped. She must have thought I could accept it given we were not happy in the marriage. She glanced up at the clock. Beyond the window gulls were sliding and slipping on a strong easterly like so many scraps of wind-blown paper.

"It's nearly four. Are you going or will I?"

The children would be at the bus stop at four.

CHRISTMAS QUIZ

My mother-in-law Muriel grew up through the Great Depression in the North-East of England. The experience of that time and of the privations of the subsequent war years left her with a strong sense of economy and an aversion to waste. If a kitchen roll was cheaper than two loo rolls she would cut it in half. She also disliked the whole idea of credit, believing you should cut your coat according to your cloth. Household bills would be paid immediately on receipt. I once suggested there was no harm is using the thirty days credit usually allowed, to which she answered that if she had had the value she would pay the price with no shilly-shallying.

During her first pregnancy her husband John did not own a car but he did have a motorcycle. As the pregnancy advanced Muriel found the growing bump prevented her occupying the pillion seat of this machine. The solution was to sit backwards, facing the way they had come, her hands somehow clasping John's hips behind her back. She was a strong and determined woman for whom the increasing affluence of post-war Britain came as a surprise and in time almost an embarrassment on her personal level.

John took early retirement to enter the ministry of the Church of England, first as a curate in Hull and then as a vicar in rural North Yorkshire. They sold the family home in Gosforth and John invested the money while they lived in a spacious country vicarage. The investments did well through the Thatcher boom years and when John sadly died of a heart attack shortly after retirement Muriel found she had financial advantages beyond her needs or wants. Part of the solution was to be generous with cash gifts to her ten grandchildren on their birthdays and at Christmas.

As the children grew away from infancy it occurred to Muriel that the distribution of the annual Christmas largesse should at least be acknowledged by some deepened awareness of what the festival was really about. She was herself a deeply religious woman of evangelical bent. She came up with the idea of a Christmas quiz, the passing of which would act as an entitlement to the Christmas cash. It started off simply enough but by the time Lizzie was ten it had progressed to a recitation from memory of the titles of all the books of the Old Testament.

There are thirty-nine books in the Protestant version and remembering them all took some doing for a young child but the stakes were high. £25 to be exact, which at the time represented something of a fortune to the recipient. The titles did not have to be recited in the right order, and the candidate could have as many repeat goes as he or she needed to pass, but all had to be named from memory. A studious atmosphere would prevail as each child faced Granny alone in whatever room was available. Everyone passed eventually but Lizzie got it at her first attempt.

Some weeks later the teacher of Lizzie's R.I. class at middle school asked the class if anyone could name one or more books of the Old Testament. Lizzie's hand shot up with obvious eagerness. 'Yes Lizzie' said the teacher whereupon Lizzie launched into a recital of all thirty-nine names as the teacher stood slack-jawed, convinced she was facing the brainwashed child of some fundamentalist nutters.

The following Christmas the children were bigger, inflation had moved things on and the prize money had been upped to £60 per person. Muriel, possibly increasingly aware of her own mortality, was determined to divest herself of as much worldly wealth as the opportunity allowed and so opened the arena to everybody in the house including adults. The house was my brother-in-law's in Scotland and with the children and diverse in-laws the total census was around thirty. If all complied with Granny's wishes she would enjoy parting with some £1800, though some adults felt their own ethics would not permit them to humour her in this way. Others faced no such obstacles.

The test, in line with the greater prize money, had increased in severity: The Ten Commandments had to be recited in the correct order and in the proper, archaic, form. This was a challenge, particularly to the younger candidates who had no idea what was being talked about. Somebody had the idea of running off thirty copies of the text as *aide-memoires*. Subsequently a mixture of children and adults could be observed moving quietly through the house and garden while holding sheets of paper, their lips moving silently as they rehearsed before submitting to Granny's vigilant listening.

After dealing with several queries as to the meaning of the various items in the text I felt wearied enough to spend most of the morning in an armchair listening to Celine Dion singing *My Heart Will Go On*. It's a good song.

NO FRILLS

Everyone knows Ryanair is a 'no frills' airline but sometimes landing in fog on the small mountain-top airfield at Knock in Co.Mayo can be 'all thrills'. Why else would passengers descending from an arriving plane hug each other and signal jubilant thumbs up towards the people watching from behind the glass of the terminal? The man with wet patches on his knees might even have kissed the tarmac.

From inside the departure lounge we had been straining our eyes into the gloom searching for the incoming plane. The thunder of its engines had waxed and waned twice as it made a couple of low-level reconnaissance passes over the runway. Finally it had loomed out of the fog to touch down with more than the usual degree of bounce and wobble. Watching the arrivals it was hard to know if the tears being shed in the arms of welcoming friends and relatives indicated love or just relief at being alive- like the Italians the Irish are not embarrassed by the expression of emotion. All this happiness at being on the ground was not encouraging for those of us waiting to board the same plane for the return flight to Stansted. Mind you, Charles and I had already been primed for problems by the check-in people.

We had been fishing on the River Moy. Charles had arrived in Ballina without waders, planning to buy a pair in the town. But Charles is big, especially his feet, which require a size 14W.

Unsurprisingly the local fishing tackle shop had no such size in stock. Nevertheless, in a spirit of optimism, its proprietor had disappeared into a jumbled storeroom with a vague recollection that as a youth he had once mistakenly ordered a giant's boots which might still be gathering dust. Then his brother arrived back from an early lunch and, learning what was being searched for, shouted in to remind him they had sold them to the local vet in 1962 to wear over his shoes when artificially inseminating cows.

Eventually Charles had been obliged to force his feet into the largest pair of waders they did have, a size 12. He then deployed a tactic familiar to those who use retail therapy: to mitigate the psychological and, in this case, physical discomfort of an unsatisfactory purchase he kept on buying. He bought a proper heavyweight fishing coat of the correct size (XXXL), a stylish wide-brimmed rain hat and numerous items of fishing tackle, including a selection of those Irish-designed salmon lures less than romantically called 'Flying Condoms'. This sudden bout of unexpected consumerism left the brothers in happy mood. For his part Charles was lighter in pocket but a good deal heavier in accoutrements and had laid the makings for our difficulties at the airport a week or so later

"That will be ninety-six euros sir." This pronouncement came from a young woman wearing an airline uniform and several millimetres of make-up. If she had kept still she could have passed for a plastic mannequin. Her lack of facial expression suggested she had not the faintest appreciation of the absurdity of demanding such an outrageous amount.

"What?!" cried Charles.

"Fifteen and a half kilos overweight sir, at six euros twenty per kilo" she offered by way of mathematically justifying this ridiculous surcharge.

"I'm not paying that- I only paid twenty-three euros for the return ticket!" spluttered Charles.

"I'm sorry sir but we are obliged to charge for baggage over twenty kilos" said Plastic Face, carefully avoiding eye contact by examining Charles's ticket, probably in the hope of discovering some error justifying another excessive charge.

At this Charles brusquely hauled the offending piece of luggage off the scales and began unpacking it just to the side of the check-in queue.

"Sir ..." Plastic Face, still without expression, leaned forward over the desk to hand him back his ticket. He reached up and snatched it rather ungraciously.

"Here put some of this stuff in your bag, you're way under twenty kilos" demanded Charles of me. The waiting passengers looked on in faint amusement as shirts, underwear, toiletries and Flying Condoms were transferred from Charles's bag to mine.

"Stop, that's enough" I objected "I'll be way over twenty now- I'm not paying for your rubbish!"

Charles, albeit with courtesy towards the other passengers, for whom he was developing empathy as fellow victims of Ryanair, inserted our two bags back into the queue and onto the scales. Mine was more or less dead on the twenty kilos allowed, but his was still a good sixty euros overweight, a large part of which was the new fishing coat.

"Bugger" he said quietly as he eyed the scales. But a a new plan dawned.

"What if I wear my fishing coat?"

"What you wear is up to you sir, the regulations do not require us to weigh the passengers" replied his tormentor. Her face remained impassive but her eyes clearly said that, if it was up to her, not only would she weigh passengers, particularly large ones, but personally disembowel any one of them if an ounce overweight. A person of sensitivity might have interpreted her comment as a pointed reference to body size but as Charles doesn't suffer from sensitivity he simply removed the case from the scales and moved to one side again.

"Right!" he exclaimed with the air of a man given authorisation to cheat.

First he took off his pullover. Then he put on two shirts from the case over the one he already had on. Then he put on his thick fishing pullover before replacing the one he had just taken off. Then a body warmer, the zip only just fastenable over all this bulk. The XXXL coat was an easy fit over the top of everything. He then crammed its pockets with various bits of fishing tackle, took off his shoes, shoved them in a cargo pocket inside the coat, and pulled on the waders. The queue, by now audibly chuckling, was moved to actual applause when, in a *coup de theatre*, Charles jammed the new fishing hat on his head. Arms and legs akimbo he now shuffled back to the check-in desk like an animated Michelin man. The admiring queue opened a wide space to admit him.

"That's eight euros overweight baggage charge sir" intoned Plastic Face glancing from passport photo to Charles's already profusely sweating body while registering no response to its alarmingly increased bulk.

"That's more like it, still too much mind" said Charles reaching for his wallet, forgetting it was now buried under several layers of clothing and wader rubber.

"Jack, give me eight euros- come on!"

I handed the money over, the bags went through and we moved on, but only briefly. Charles had not thought ahead as far as security.

Airport security staff, faced with someone sweating heavily, cannot be sure whether the discomfort arises from impending martyrdom or simply innocent over-dressing. So they remain calm but insistent. Knock-Stansted is probably an unlikely route for a terrorist to target and Charles looks an unlikely terrorist but then evil-doers get more devious by the day. Everything had to come off down to the socks and all pockets emptied. This de-construction of Charles's outfit, followed by its reclamation took a tedious amount of time but eventually we proceeded into the departure lounge with armfuls of surplus clothing and no little amount of fishing gear. What followed was the unsettling scenario previously described as the incoming plane rocked and rolled down through the fog.

Once aboard we were pleasantly surprised to find our seats were those facing the forward bulkhead. A favoured position with ample legroom for Charles, although most of it was taken up by the fishing coat and waders etc'. At that point a flight attendant, looking suspiciously like a twin sister of Plastic Face and definitely a graduate of the same customer relations school, told Charles very firmly that all unsecured items had to be placed in the overhead luggage compartments before take-off. This was easier said than done because the compartments above us revealed themselves to be crammed with various bits of emergency kit and those further aft were filled to brimming with the luggage of other passengers. No, Face Two said, there was nowhere else, crew space was severely restricted and had to be maintained clutter free. She added, unnecessarily I thought, that we should have checked in anything not wanted on the flight. For once Charles sensibly decided not to charge a red rag.

She then helpfully concluded there was no alternative but for Charles to put everything back onto his person again. It was either that, she said, with a manner presumably honed on difficult passengers, or throw the stuff out onto the tarmac. It was unfortunate for Charles that the plane then sat on the tarmac for nearly an hour waiting for the fog to thin a little. The cabin temperature steadily rose into the eighties. It wouldn't have been so bad if they had turned on the air-conditioning, but then it's a 'no-frills' airline.

MEET AND DELETE

"How did you two meet?" If the truthful answer is 'online' most post-millenium couples would be happy to say so. It's as if it's evidence of their being in tune with the times. It was not always so: at its outset computer dating carried a stigma that would have had them lying. The connotations were not so good in those early days: Thai brides by mail order, seedy middle-aged men, desperate no-hopers and sexual predators. Yet the potential of the internet for making connections was obvious. It put the world at your feet, or at least at your fingertips, and ever greater numbers of 'normal' people were using it to widen their search for partners. In 2002 I had been divorced three years and wondered if I should give it a go. My divorcee friend Felicity was an expert. She was looking for someone tall and handsome, so there was no risk of things getting too personal when she offered to talk me through her technique.

"Scroll down until your eye catches someone you like the look of. Read their profile but don't believe any of it. Or the photo for that matter, it will be years old. If you're not put off make contact- you'll have to go through the site to begin with. Get their phone number or e-mail, or give yours, and as soon as you can, talk on the phone. Then you'll know if there's any mileage in it. Nine times out of ten there won't be. But if you're still not put off arrange a meeting straight away. Then you can delete them. Because ninety-nine times out of a hundred it'll be a dead end. They'll weigh twenty stone or live with twenty cats or be train-spotters or failed suicides. If you can conclude the whole process in 48 hours so much the better. What you definitely do not want to do is to make a big investment in e-mails or repeat phone calls because inevitably you're expectations will grow. Then when they're dashed you'll feel emotionally drained. 'Meet and delete', believe me, it's the only way."

"But if you delete everyone what's the point?"

"It's like the premium bonds, you always hope for the million even if all you ever get is a tenner."

I wasn't too sure exactly how that analogy worked.

Eustacia phoned me first. I was rather taken with the name and the voice. It probably wasn't a good idea to have asked her if her name was something to do with toothpaste.

"That's Euthymol" she said back crisply "I think it's medicinal stuff for people with false teeth. You haven't got false teeth have you?"

"Hang on, let me turn up my hearing aid so I can hear you" She laughed. At least she had a sense of humour I thought, not knowing at that point quite how reliant on it I would be.

Following Felicity's instructions as closely as possible, I asked her if she would be able to meet me the following evening. She couldn't, but she could the next, a Tuesday. The question was where. Eustacia lived fifteen miles south of Ipswich and I live twenty miles north, so the obvious place was Ipswich. But all the town pubs we could think of were large and noisy. A country pub would be better: subdued lighting, an open fire and quiet corners. I suggested the Ramsholt Arms, a cosy pub in a picturesque setting on the River Deben about ten miles east of Ipswich. Not that the setting would matter too much as it was January and it would be pitch dark by five. On reflection it was a strange choice and probably a bit thoughtless.

Anyone who has been to the Ramsholt Arms will know it's in a fairly remote location easiest to get to by boat. By road several miles of narrow lanes twisting and bending towards the coast eventually get you to a long straight track, seemingly going nowhere, that finally dumps you on the riverside next to the pub. This was all pre-satnav so I gave Eustacia detailed directions.

Driving down the track to the river I was struck by how dark and black a night it was. Not a lighted window anywhere and no other traffic. Well, I thought, at least the pub should be nice and quiet on a weekday evening: it can get pretty rammed at weekends. This thought gave way to an unpleasant but growing premonition. Lights should have been visible by now. Horrified by the situation I realised I had unwittingly engineered I pulled up beside the darkened pub. It was as black and deserted as the miles of empty country surrounding it. Nobody actually lives down there. The only sound came from the winter treetops rattling in the breeze overhead and the tide slurping and sucking past the jetty, invisible in the dark. The night was as black as ink. If I had been a regular habitué of the Arms I would have known that in winter it opens only at weekends.

Mortified I reversed into the car park and waited, careful to leave my sidelights on. It couldn't have looked worse. Nor could I ring Eustacia to explain, I only had her landline number on my phone. I reasoned she was unlikely to show up anyway- a sensible woman would have turned back miles before she ever got this far. But on the other hand I had warned her it was a bit out of the way.

Very close to the appointed hour headlights began to play up and down the trees as a car approached. I jumped out and hurried to intercept the vehicle, a flood of apologies ready. Dazzled by the oncoming headlights I waited. The car stopped beside me and the driver's window lowered. Giving me a quizzical look was a uniformed policeman. A second one sat beside him.

"Everything all right sir?" asked the driver.

"Well, yes, sort of. Didn't realise the pub was shut."

"Weekends only in winter sir."

"Yes I know that now, but I arranged to meet someone here."

"Ah. This will be them now then," he said.

Another pair of headlights was approaching down the track. I realised the situation now looked even worse than it had a minute earlier. I walked back to meet this second vehicle. The window rolled down. This was Eustacia.

To an onlooker the lights of our three cars clustered beside the river would have given the impression of some sort of 'situation' going down. The drama was now heightened by the policeman in the passenger seat of the patrol car getting out and scanning the ebbing tide with a hand-held searchlight.

"Hello, you must be Eustacia." I said stupidly.

"Yes. And you're Jack. What's going on?"

"I'm really sorry but the pub's closed. I didn't realise it's winter."

"You didn't realise it's winter?" She was looking at me in an incredulous way. "Why are the police here?"

"I've no idea. They just showed up. Really I'm not a serial murderer or a rapist. I haven't done anything."

The second policeman was now back in the patrol car. It swung around in a circle and came back towards us. The window was still down as it stopped alongside.

"Just checking the jetty. It's a popular spot to land illegals at night," explained the driver, "someone reported seeing lights down here."

"That was probably me. The lights I mean" I said.

"Probably. But you two are not meeting anyone from Afghanistan are you? Have a good evening."

I think he was smirking as he drove off.

"Eustacia I am so sorry about this. I'm an idiot. The nearest pub's at Shottisham, a couple of miles. They must be open. Will you follow me there?"

"It's probably a better bet than staying here" she answered without smiling. Clearly there was a lot of ground to make up.

At each junction we passed I fully expected her headlights to disappear as she aborted the evening and made a run for home. As to whether The Sorrel Horse would actually be open I had no idea. I couldn't remember the last time I'd been in it, or even past it. Village pubs were closing all the time. What I did know was that my embryonic relationship with Eustacia would not weather another failure.

The Horse was open but only just. This was before it changed hands to become an attractive 'destination' pub. The outside sign was unlit and only a dim glow showed from a grubby window. In a Hardy novel it might have suggested romance or mystery but the reality was just dingy. We parked outside and I used the light from my phone to light our way to the door. It opened onto a palpable silence as you might experience going into a crypt. But our entry was as actors onto a stage, albeit before a small audience. Two old men stood at the bar, both in flat caps. If they had been conversing before the door moved it's opening stopped them dead as they waited to see who might appear from behind it. We approached the bar. An unshaven barman appeared from a room at the rear, greeted us without enthusiasm and took up a rather confrontational pose in front of us. He gave the impression that the sooner he could get back to whatever it was he had been doing the better he would like it.

Eustacia asked for a glass of red wine. They only sold wine by the bottle the barman said. Nor did he have any elderflower cordial but yes, he did have sparkling water. Ice and lemon was not offered so Eustacia asked for some. With an air of great weariness he lumbered off to a kitchen somewhere at the back. We heard the fridge door bang and ice cubes rattle into a bucket. When he returned I ordered a half of lager. Our audience further along the bar observed these exchanges in silence. Presumably the presence of strangers was of greater interest than whatever they might have been discussing before we came in. Feeling like a pair of Pakistanis at a National Front meeting we carried our drinks to a corner table that we hoped might be out of direct sightline from the bar.

Eustacia was rather nice, slim and petite with blonde hair tied up in a bun. I was grateful she showed no outward sign of irritation at my incompetence. She wore small dangly earrings, a black knee length skirt and matching cashmere top. Probably the most glamorous thing The Horse had seen for weeks, possibly ever. I wondered if this might be the worst date she had ever been involved in. But before I could ask her her mobile phone rang. Half raising a hand to signal apology, she answered it. She listened for a few moments without speaking and then with some more complicated hand signals indicated she was going outside to talk. I wondered if this was a clever ruse she had set up with a friend to extricate herself from awkward dating situations. I expected her to return to say she was sorry but that she would have to rush off to attend to a sick child or aged mother.

She was gone a long time. As the minutes rolled by I drank some lager, looked at my phone, toyed with the beer mat and noticed the two old men at the bar had resumed talking to one another. After fifteen minutes or so I wondered if I should take Eustacia's drink out to her, though icy water didn't seem much comfort on a chilly winter's night. Anyway it might be intrusive. I waited. After half an hour I wondered if she had gone, so I got up and looked out of the window. She was still on the phone just beside the door. I tried to recall if this was the worst date I had ever been involved in. At which point Eustacia came back in, sat down and took a sip of her water. Sitting back she went "Phew" as if inviting inquiry into whatever had just transpired.

"Trouble?" I asked.

"No, just business. But it can be wearing."

"Oh. What sort of business do you do?"

"Undertaking."

Eustacia was not the first undertaker I had met socially but she was the first female one. She told me she was one of the few 'green' ones in East Anglia, specialising in cardboard coffins and woodland burials, 'that sort of thing'. The phone call had been from a living client she said.

"A relative you mean?"

"No, an imminent suicide."

"What?"

"A woman who wanted to have all the arrangements in place before she went. In endless detail. She's weaving a coffin from willow she's collected from along the River Waveney."

"Did she *say* she was going to kill herself?"

"No, but you get so you can tell."

"Good grief, shouldn't you inform the police or a relative or something?"

"You can't. It would be a betrayal of trust."

"Well yes, but shouldn't you try to talk them out of it, or at least put the Samaritans onto them?"

"You're forgetting I'm an undertaker!"

We laughed darkly at that. I bought her a gin and tonic to help cheer her up and avoid the barman wasting the rest of the ice and lemon. I apologised again for my ridiculous choice of venues but then couldn't help throwing in a pun about her being used to funereal locations. That might have been the last straw because we didn't meet again. But when the time comes, and if she's still in business, I would be very happy to.

ANOTHER HOLE
STORY

Another house, another time, another drainage problem.
The outfall from the on-going barn conversion at Reckford Farm was half a metre below the connection to the
sewage main in the road. The choice was to install an independent digester system or simply a tank fitted with a pump to lift
the stuff high enough to get it into the sewer. The latter was
cheaper.

The tank required a hole, quite a big, deep hole because
the manufacturers observe the building regulation that insists
you must have enough storage for two days. This is in case the
power to the pump fails and you flood your house with your
own waste. It takes a decent sized mini-digger to dig a hole ten
feet deep and six feet in diameter but I hired one, got the tank on
site and set to with Mick and Percy. When you've dug the hole
you have to pour slurry concrete into the bottom to set around
the base of the empty tank. Otherwise it will pop up out of the
ground like a cork in a bath, particularly if the site is wet which
ours was.

By midday we had the hole dug and were ready for the
next stage. Mick and Percy set off in their Transit truck to collect some wet concrete from our local ready-mix plant. I took
the opportunity for a lunch break. We had dug the hole inside a
small grass enclosure that was home to Spam and Beans, the two
pet pigs. Although pigs are very intelligent moving them from

one place to another can be a slow and sometimes frustrating operation, so I had left them where they were. I assured Mick and Percy that pigs are far too sensible to go near a deep hole. They were doubtful but I was confident and went off to lunch, failing to appreciate that pigs, like cats, sometimes allow curiosity to overwhelm caution. Unlike cats, however, they have a fairly extreme body mass index but absolutely no idea of its implications.

Reappearing after about half an hour I approached the hole just in time to see Beans coming towards it from the opposite direction. I broke into a run waving my arms and shouting "No! No! No!" More or less at the same moment the lip of the hole gave way under Beans' considerable weight. He did a sort of slow motion backward somersault before disappearing below ground level. A large black pig upside down in mid-air is not something you see very often outside old Monty Python reruns. Reaching the hole I realised why Beans had been so intent on looking into it- Spam was already in the bottom. Now the two pigs were circling and jostling each other like two fat men at the bottom of a well.

At this point Mick and Percy returned with the concrete and for several minutes hilarity prevented the mounting of a rescue attempt. Yet the situation was serious- at any moment the walls of the hole could collapse with fatal consequences. This realisation spurred us into action. Percy climbed into the digger and pulled out a sloping ramp from the side of the hole in the hope that the pigs would be able to clamber out. But they were too fat and the soil was too soft. They tried but just kept sliding back to the bottom of the hole that was now a goo of liquid mud and the malodorous evidence of their terror. We would have to somehow get a strap around them and lift them out one at a time with the digger. They were my pigs and it was my fault so there was no question as to who had to get in the hole.

I jumped down onto their backs setting them off in a new frenzy of squealing. The most extreme mud wrestling is as nothing compared to sharing a six-foot diameter hole with two panicked pigs. Apparently mud covered women are somehow supposed to be sexy, the same can't be said for pigs. Getting straps under their wide bellies at the bottom of a mud-hole would be a challenge for the most unhinged reality show. The real possibility that the struggle might at any moment bring down tons of wet earth to entomb man and pigs in a communal grave would add ample drama.

Eventually I was able to give a thumbs up to Percy on the digger and there went Beans mid-air again, but this time the right way up. Then it was Spam's turn. I crawled out of the hole looking like a TV news shot of a barely-alive survivor just dug from a mudslide. This prompted another break for hilarity. Meanwhile, having instantly recovered their phlegm, Beans and Spam ambled away rooting and snuffling, quite unconcerned by my vocal renouncing of their intelligence.

Then we realised that the concrete had started to go off so we had to dump it and go for another lot.

SUSPECT!

T hrough the winter of 2007/8 my daughter Holly was living in Budapest as a participant in the 'Erasmus' academic program. Invited to visit I bought a ticket from Ryanair for mid-January. It was an evening flight that meant I could get in nearly a full day's pruning on the farm before leaving. January 2008 was cold in England but I knew it would be a lot colder in central Europe so it seemed sensible to drive to Stansted straight from work still in my warm winter work clothes.

Despite squally snow flurries and the panicky media warnings attendant on forecasts of more I arrived at the Ryanair desk just in time to check in before its notorious forty minute pre-flight cut-off came into operation. I moved on to the queue for security and shot a quick glance at the notices prohibiting nail varnish, toothpaste, shampoo and other seemingly innocuous items capable of blowing up an aeroplane if in the wrong hands. And once again, as in so many security queues before, I groaned at my incompetence in forgetting the pocket knife in my jeans pocket. I keep it there, which is why they are called 'pocket' knives (how did they arrive at 'pocket' battleship I wonder?). Being a farmer I'm always in need of a knife for something or other. Over the years I've had to throw away probably more than a dozen as a result of forgetting to tuck them into my bag at airport check-ins. Most often they have been those reasonably cheap wooden-handled French knives called Opinel. But this one was different. A posh Swiss army knife that a Bulgarian student on the farm had bought for me after disdainfully noticing the French one I had been using. I really did not want to leave it in the dump box with oversized tubs of face cream and body lotion.

I left the queue and approached a young man in a stripey cardboard hat just shutting up a Krispy Kreme doughnut stall.

"Sorry, we're closed" he said without even looking up.

"No," I said "I don't want a doughnut but you must have a kitchen utensils draw. Couldn't you just stick this in it for now and I'll pick it up later in the week."
I knew it was a long shot. He looked at the knife and then at me.

"Sorry mate" he said as he carried on clearing away the doughnuts, not so matey after all.

I approached a group of four men in yellow jackets chatting together, obviously airport staff of some sort.
"Excuse me" I said and explained my predicament.

"Lost luggage, over there mate" said one, nodding toward the distant end of the terminal.
I'd already thought of that but judged the £5 minimum charge made the idea unviable. I said as much.

"If I were you then mate," said another of the men "I'd go out to the short-term car park and tuck it down a rabbit hole. Just remember which one."
A lot of rabbits live at Stansted airport. That did seem a good idea so I thanked this more matey mate and set off to find a quiet part of the car park.

Leaving the far end of the terminal building in the dark I noticed a steel footbridge over a railway line. On balance this seemed a better bet for a safe hiding place than a rabbit hole. After all a rabbit might chew my knife, bury it, or drag it away. I wormed into a space below the bridge and was stretching up to deposit the knife inside the lip of the highest RSJ I could reach when I must have triggered a sensor somewhere. Suddenly lots of lights came on and a woman wearing a high-vis vest over a sort of suit-cum-uniform was running from the terminal towards me. She carried a clipboard and a hand-held radio.

"What are you doing?' she demanded in a high-pitched voice not far short of panic.

"It's OK," I said, "just hiding a knife."

"Oh my god!" she exclaimed.

I could see two large men, also high-vis, running from inside the terminal. They were halted momentarily by the languorous operation of the automatic doors. Squeezing through sideways as the opening widened they ran on towards us. One took up a position behind me, the other stood next my interrogator. She seemed calmed by the arrival of this back-up. She reached forward and took the knife from my hand.

"Follow me" she barked as she led our group of four back towards the terminal.

"Look" I said, determined to sound as relaxed and non-threatening as possible "it's no big deal, you can just throw it away if you like."

"It's too late for that!" she snapped before speaking into her radio.

"Male suspect detained hiding a knife- request armed support."

I thought this all a bit over-dramatic but meekly followed her through the terminal to a sort of open kiosk labelled SECURITY. Our two-man bodyguard departed.

"Wait there" instructed the clipboard woman as she took up a standing position a couple of yards away from me.

Wondering how the time was going in relation to my flight departure I felt for my phone in the pocket of my heavy outdoor jacket. What my fingers encountered was the familiar cylindrical heft of a loaded 12-bore cartridge. I thought it best to play it straight whatever the consequences.

"You probably aren't going to like this either," I said, proffering the cartridge, holding it vertically between my thumb and forefinger.

"What is it?" my guard asked.

"A shotgun cartridge" I answered.

She took it from my hand and turned it over.

"Oh my god it's live!" she exclaimed in a voice reverting back towards hysteria.

Then, regaining some official-like composure, she spoke into her radio.

"Urgent! Security! The knifeman is carrying live weapons ammunition!"

Budapest was starting to look a distant dream.

COVER

My friend Sammy got married while still a teenager and was divorced by twenty-one. There was no house or child and the lawyers took most of the cash so Sammy went travelling on the cheap. When she came back she worked at whatever job presented itself for she's a sociable girl with lots of contacts, including a boyfriend who makes drums from African goatskins. She is a knowledgeable plantswoman and a good cook. She goes to music gigs and occasionally runs in marathons. She came twenty-third of the women in the 1998 Moscow Marathon.

By the time she was thirty-five Sammy had put enough aside for the deposit on a semi-detached farmworkers' cottage on the edge of the old airfield. As a vegetarian, she lives there frugally, keeping a productive garden but the house is always cold. It's north facing with only an open fire in the front room and a paraffin stove in the tiny kitchen. The roof leaks and she rarely turns on the immersion heater for the luxury of hot water. She runs an old Renault van but financially her first concern each month is to make the mortgage payment on her house. After paying it there is not always a great deal left so Sammy is always reluctant to pay out for any unnecessary extras. A necessary one is the house insurance the mortgage company insists she keeps up to date.

She recently contacted her insurers to check all was in order, which it was, but before hanging up the lady on the other end of the phone said

"I notice you don't have any contents insurance."

"I don't think I need it" replied Sammy.

"You'd be surprised how much it might cost to replace things, even after a minor accident" said the lady "what about your three-piece suite?"

"I haven't got one" said Sammy.

"Well you must have a sofa surely. They cost a fortune now."

"I found mine on the side of the road" countered Sammy "and the chair came from the dump."

"Well, have you got a hi-fi system, a computer, or a television?"

"No" said Sammy. This was true, although a friend had promised her an old PC.

"Oh," said the insurance representative with a tone of patronising sympathy "nothing then?"

At this point Sammy began to feel embarrassed that she was lacking in so many of the items that would have qualified her as a mainstream member of the consumer society. She flailed about in her mind for something with which to restore her credibility with her interrogator.

"Well, there is my camera."

"Ah," said the insurance lady "what's that worth?"

"Not very much."

"Ten thousand is the minimum cover under our contents policy, but it will cover everything for under forty pounds a year"

So Sammy signed up.

When she told me about this insurance conversation I was surprised that she had such a valuable camera. I had never seen her with it.

"How much is it worth?" I asked.

"Oh, I haven't got one," said Sammy "I just felt so embarrassed at not having any of the things she asked about."

"So you've insured something you haven't got?"

"Afraid so."

I think there must be a moral hidden in this somewhere, but I'm not clever enough to work out what it is.

ACKNOWLEDGEMENT

These stories would not exist of course were it not for the characters in them. They are, or were, all real people who I have subjected to some degree or other of artistic licence in their description. I sincerely hope that by doing so I have not caused offence. If I have I apologise, that was certainly not my intention. Rather I am grateful to them all for making my time such a rich experience.

ABOUT THE AUTHOR

Jack Rosenthal

Born of a G.I. bride in 1947 Jack Rosenthal schooled in Norfolk and Arizona before working for the Forestry Commission in Yorkshire. In 1979 he took up asparagus farming on the Suffolk coast where he now lives. He has three daughters.

BOOKS BY THIS AUTHOR

Letters From An Airfield

'It was if they came from another planet' reflected one Suffolk farm worker remembering the arrival of the 'Yanks' in 1944. 'They took the place by storm!' recalled an old lady - with a twinkle in her eye because, more than the place, it was the young women they took. The tall, courteous, big-spending strangers often became the first love and sometimes the love of a life. In "Letters from an Airfield", Jack Rosenthal tells the story of one such romance, particularly significant to him as he would become its offspring. Using letters preserved by his mother, Rosenthal reconstructs the relationship from the day of its beginning in March 1944, to its culmination in marriage in July 1945. With the stories behind linked weddings the narrative ranges from a dramatic escape after the fall of Hong Kong to the nightmares of the Arctic convoys and is supported by lively insights into the histories and social circumstances of the four families involved.

From Sea To Sea

An entertaining and light-hearted account of a 66-year-old's 51-day walk/climb in the Pyrenees from the Atlantic Ocean to the Mediterranean Sea following the famous French walking route, the GR10. Tips on preparation, how to avoid falling into a crevasse and when not to ignore the guidebook are some of the many things Jack should have brushed up on before he set out. Yet he managed it, with the help of occasional odd-ball companions, French restaurateurs and Spanish garage owners (he hadn't realised he'd wandered into Spain). Anyone planning to embark on this demanding trek will find Jack's account invaluable, while everyone can share with him the ups and downs of the adventure, the eccentricities of the French and the joy of accomplishing a lifelong ambition.

Printed in Great Britain
by Amazon

83992525R00130